my Labor Pains were Worse than Yours

PRESS AHEAD PRESS

an imprint of
Rope Swing Publishing

"When women raise each other up, they all rise together. You don't need your name under their successes to still be a part of them; like a silent partner in business you still reap the benefits."

–James Sherrill Epperson
7/17/1932 – 11/21/2011

Foreword from the Publisher

Content warnings are important as they can prevent someone from reading material that may be disturbing or unsettling to them. This book contains chapters from different women that include material that may be sensitive and of a violent nature.

My Labor Pains Were Worse Than Yours
Breaking the strongholds of societal independence

ISBN: 978-1-954058-10-1 (paperback)
ISBN: 978-1-954058-11-8 (ebook)

Starting Anew

Michelle Jester

It never fails. We're all sitting together in a circle awaiting the soon-to-be mother who is demurely opening one gift after another, prolonging the baby shower by at least thirty minutes.

It usually starts there.

One woman sparks the same conversation you hear at every single baby shower with a few words, "My labor was..."

Followed by the next contestant when they add, "Well, my labor was considered *heavy labor.*"

After attending so many baby showers over the years, what one wants to say is, "You are all horrible people."

Instead what you find yourself saying is, "Well, my labor lasted for nineteen hours." Adding, "With no pain meds."

"Well, I breast fed for the first full year."

"I used only cloth diapers."

"I cradle hugged."

What it all boils down to is *who, truly, is the better mom here? The better woman?*

I have not only witnessed it, I have regrettably been a part of it. And we justify it as sharing our stories or maybe even trying to relate to one another. Instead, what it does is isolate some women.

I couldn't breastfeed our son, not for lack of trying. Thankfully my mother was there for the first few days and she reassured me that bottle feeding was okay; feeding, was the most important part. Still, I thought of all the mom groups I was in at the time. I was feeling so uncomfortable with my role as a mom, so I clung to every word I could. One of the newest trends then, and I say trend because it really was one, that you could not bottle feed. I was told that not only was it bad for your baby, but bottle-feeding was bad for your body as well. While breastfeeding has always been *the best way,* all the groups then agreed that bottle-feeding had become a no-no. To add, *what good mom wouldn't put in the effort and deal with the pain to have a healthier child?* The talk of bonding while you fed your child, single-handedly, or in this case, single-breastedly, sounded so endearing that I knew, without a doubt, I would breastfeed.

If I could do nothing else right, I'd do that.

Our son had other ideas, and breastfeeding was definitely not one of them. Credit to the nuns who tried over and over to help him and me "get it," but in the end, I bottle-fed.

Like I said, thankfully my mom was there.

Once I had stopped participating in the conversation at baby showers, I noticed it's not "Me too!" banter, it's "But I!" banter.

Since then, I have realized there are questions I'll never find a definitive answer to.

When exactly were women pitted against one another?

When were we compared so strongly that we started to negate another woman's journey?

Unfortunately, in all of our lives we have had other women that try to tear us down. Maybe we were *that* woman at times, too.

3

Why would women try to hurt other women, when what we need to be doing is helping one another?

I first started noticing competition and jealousy in grade school. There was one early bloomer, that before her breasts started growing, was one of the well-liked ones. After she started flourishing and gaining the attention of the boys, she became the enemy. Now, maybe that was simply human nature, to thrive and survive, but I remember some of the other girls were merciless. The boys didn't help by publicly making comments about either how great she looked, or how slow all the other girls were getting their lady parts. I thought often how lonely that beautiful, early bloomer looked, instead of happy about being the first "woman" in school. Then, she started hanging out with the boys at recess, laughing and lightly flirting. She still didn't have many girl-friends, but she had plenty of boy ones. Once the other girls started showing their signs of womanhood, she gained a few friends back.

Since then, I've had a daughter and was forced to watch the same circumstances repeated through her group of friends as well. It's when the group split into two, then three, smaller groups. I noticed the boys group didn't really split until later in high school, and even then most of them remained friendly.

After speaking at a woman's conference nearly thirty years ago, and experiencing firsthand how calloused adult women could be, it brought back a memory from my youth. We were visiting my Aunt Gail. She always had the best books and memorabilia from our family. She had boxes of old pictures, poems, and letters.

Hours of sifting through boxes of miscellaneous family letters my grandmother and Aunt Gail had acquired through the years, I found several examples that will always stay with me. I jotted down notes off of the letters onto notebook paper and never really did much with them. At the time I was young, unmarried, and really didn't know what to do with some of the things I read. However, I have held onto those notes for years.

One was a letter from a mother to her daughter. In it the mother stated that the father had received a missive from the daughter's new husband. The writing was difficult to read, but what I could read was that the daughter's husband had said that "the townsmen hurried that her [daughter's] work was not as ample as the other townswomen." The mother went on to explain that it reflected badly on her family name and her father wanted relayed that she should try "solidly to meet with the standard of the women in her new town" lest she "be a recluse among them." Her mother went on to state her hopes were that during the time it would take for the letter to reach her [daughter] that it "will not have seen you shunned already." The mother ended with "tender instruct" that her daughter should "strive improvement over those around you, or thus you may fall into disuse and be discarded."

In the same file was a return letter, dated a little under five months later, her daughter told of how she had worked as "hard as was instructed" and can "with a jovial heart state now earned the appraisal of the townsmen…" she added that sadly she had "quizzically, earned the scolding of many townswomen in respect to the same." She told her mother that she knew she would "ever be striving above in her work as to not be cast aside in disuse, dishonor."

As a young girl, reading these letters, *I cried.*

I cried at these exchanges. My Aunt Gail said that there were two additional letters between them, but I couldn't find those in the boxes. She said that the daughter's life never much improved. She found herself tired, alone, unhappy, and dismayed at her own life.

To realize that women were pitted against one another to help them reach a higher standard of serving men's purposes hurt me deeply. Be clear, I am not a man-hater. I adore my husband and respect many amazing men in my life, and those men respect me in return.

This book is not about them.

It is about us. *The women.*

The ones who want to break the cycle—to encourage other women to be their best self—to share their own story of trials and triumphs. Most importantly, to let other women know that, in the wise words of my dad, *when we raise each other up, we all rise together.*

There is no need to degrade, demolish, or hurt others to be our best. In addition, there is no need to not be our best in fear of overshadowing someone else. There is definitely no need to compare, because truly God made each of us differently, and we each have a mighty purpose to fill all the needs in society ... and to help other women achieve *their* best as well.

In this book you will read personal accounts from beautiful women who fill roles as homemakers, journalists, photographers, actresses, models, body builders and fitness instructors, business owners, public relations consultants, finance managers, bartenders, bloggers and podcasters, authors, marketing managers, engineers, college students and retirees, counselors and case managers, insurance agents, security analysts, and ex-military.

Some are just starting out, some are holding steady, others are starting anew ... and we all play a vital part in our world.

God bless.

Maybe

Megan Taunton

Fear is something I have dealt with for most of my life. As a woman in her late thirties, I can look back and see how much of my life was planned around fear. And when I say planned around, I mean that literally. I planned to avoid certain situations because of the fear of what could happen. I would cause myself anxiety by playing over every different scenario I thought could happen. Wondering what I would do if each situation occurred.

Sounds exhausting, right?

When I first started driving as a teenager we were hammered with the safety of driving the speed limits, using seat belts, all the norms. But I can remember some days I would go over in my mind every scenario if I were to wreck my car ... maybe if I skidded off the road I would react this way or that way. Maybe if I hydroplaned, I would do this or that. Maybe if I was stuck inside my wrecked vehicle I would...

Sounds completely irrational to many of you, but it was a legitimate fear of mine to wreck. I had experienced a lot of death in my younger years—kids dying in car accidents in my small town—so I knew it was something that could happen. If someone I cared about was driving long distances or driving in bad weather, I would worry and pray the entire time with a pit in my stomach.

When I got my first apartment, alone in another city to attend college, there were many sleepless nights I would think I heard someone downstairs, and often visualize how I would fight off an attacker. Double and triple checking door locks and always feeling uneasy alone. I sometimes wondered how I didn't pass out from the fear. Now it's good to be cautious of your surroundings, but there's also being unreasonably cautious, and that was me. Why

I ever thought I could successfully live alone is unknown to me now, especially given I had no coping strategies to help me with my fear and anxiety.

When I became pregnant for the fourth time, finally hearing and seeing a strong healthy heartbeat on the screen, it wasn't enough to relieve my fears. There was a huge part of me that feared another miscarriage. I read all the pregnancy books and desperately tried to do everything by the book—eat the right amount of calories, watch my stress, take my vitamins—but I was still looking for the other foot to drop.

I would still show up to appointments to see our baby on the ultrasound and wait for words, "something is wrong." I did little-to-no exercise for fear of causing harm to my child that I prayed for, and when I could see her growing in my belly, I still had fear. A part of my mind still screamed at me saying, *don't get too comfortable.*

In the midst of motherhood it's true what they say, fears become real. We love these little humans so much and want what's best for them, but we also fear for them. We fear them getting hurt or sick, and of course a parent's worst fear is losing a child.

I remember when my first child was nine

months old and she started running a fever. Her temperature reached 104 degrees, and I literally flipped out; she had been given meds, but I just knew she was dying, so I scooped her up and rushed to the emergency room. Needless to say, when we got there and they checked her temperature, it was down. I remember feeling so ridiculous and out of control. I allowed fear to consume me in that moment instead of taking a deep breath, and paying attention to how my child was acting, which was normal. That day, she was okay, just a viral infection that needed to run its course.

With this same child, years later, a diagnosis would bring out all those illogical and uncontrollable fears I had inside of me in the worst way possible.

She was diagnosed with terminal brain cancer.

All my control was gone. No scenario prepared me for that. There was no amount of me planning to avoid a situation that would get us out of what we were in.

I recently heard something that stuck with me and made me say, "Yes that's me now."

"It's okay to feel fear, but I don't live in it."

I'd had to learn this the hard way. I have lived in fear nearly my entire life, until just a few years ago. I was immersed in it so deeply that I was missing out on life; I was missing out on a vibrant and fulfilling life. Fear had kept me from ambitions, goals, experiences, friendships, and opportunities.

Fear is present and that's exactly how the devil likes it. He wants us fearful and unstable all of the time; he wants us weighed down with anxiety. He wants us to be doubtful of our God, who says He is always with us.[1] God didn't say He was sometimes with us when it was convenient or when we think He is; no ... He is always with us. I learned that letting go of full control, getting out of the driver's seat of your life and your kids' lives and allowing God to is way more fulfilling, as well as a much smoother ride.

I often criticize my younger self and think, *why didn't you just trust Him?* I sometimes wonder what I could have accomplished in my teens or my twenties if fear hadn't kept me stuck. Maybe God allowed it so I could get to this point where I am today and say these things to you. Maybe you are reading this and can relate. Maybe it's what you will need to finally let go of fear.

Maybe is a word that used to paralyze me. Now, it isn't the fear-driven word I used to hang onto; now, it's a faith-driven word I use in simply not knowing the answer, but knowing my God.

God tells us many times in the Bible to not fear, to be more like Jesus. You deserve a life that isn't weighted down by the fears of this world. You were made in His image. Not to say that you won't feel fear, we all do, but it's what you do in the fear that matters.

Do you give into it, or do you trust God with your situation?

Believe me, take the step. It seems so impossible, until you accept that you truly have no control anyway, except over your own actions. Then ... maybe, just maybe, after you accept, you will step into the power of the Holy Spirit and become the warrior you were made to be!

1. Deuteronomy 31:6*

*see scriptures in appendix, pgs 347-351

Baggage of the Past

Brittany Edwards

Most people look at their past as a burden or "baggage," something they went through, but can't seem to get over. While I agree that a good part of my past is a burden, I also choose see the beauty in it. My oldest daughter is a huge piece of my past. She is from my first marriage to my high school sweetheart. We hastily got married, and soon after, I became pregnant. Our relationship had been in a bad place for years, even before we got married. So as difficult as it was, as soon as I gathered enough strength to leave, I did. We separated when I was six months pregnant, and divorced a year later, but the beautiful blessing that came from that marriage is all I need to stay positive about my past.

For me, my oldest daughter is proof that my past isn't only a burden, but also a blessing. I strongly believe I had to walk that path in order to get to where I am now, even though it was a long, rough path, with no shortcuts. Because of that, I now know how love is supposed to feel, and I know that love isn't meant to hurt. It's meant to heal.

And when the love is right, it will heal.

My husband, three daughters, and son are proof of that. My husband's love for our oldest daughter is proof that love knows no bounds. So, do I regret my failed marriage? No, I don't regret it. I can't regret it. But I did let go of it. I had to toss that baggage in the trash, because it was of no use to me anymore. I had to let go of what could have been and move on. I also had to recognize that the only way to do that was to first *unpack* my baggage and sort it all out. It may be painful, but it is worth it.

I'm at a place in my life now where most of my past doesn't weigh heavily on me anymore. I am free from all the pain it caused my family and me. I threw all that old, heavy baggage away, and have learned to keep only the ones I can carry, because honestly I continue to make mistakes, as we all do. I hope to hold on to the baggage that reminds me of the beauty in my path, not the turbulence, because those are the ones that matter. Those are the ones you should carry with you. However, I can't say that I never think about my past, it's all around me. When I look at my baby girl, I can see it, right there on her beautiful face. But I also see that my entire past is less important than the future it brings.

My past isn't just seven years of a painful relationship; my past is so much more and just like yours, my past encompasses time as close as yesterday. My past is freeing myself from a marriage that could have ruined my daughter's life, and my past is now being married to my best friend, who stands by my side through all of it.

So now, when it comes to baggage, I keep the life lessons my journey teaches me, but I get rid of everything else. I let go of the pain from my first marriage, and keep the life-changing knowledge and experience. I let go of feeling like a failure, which I'm sure I'll address again and again. I realize that my first marriage may have failed, and I may continue to make mistakes, however, my daughter and my marriage now prove that, with God, I can win when I can learn to let go.

So, I learned to pack light.

In My Skin

Sara Simoneaux

I'm twelve years old with teeth that are too big for my face. My hair is boy-short and frizzy. I am self-conscious and uncomfortable in my own skin. For a twelve-year-old it doesn't take much. However, at twelve it's difficult to understand that we are all supposed to be different from one another.

I am self-conscious and uncomfortable in my own skin.

I'm fifteen with hair that is now long, but still frizzy and difficult to manage. I've finally grown into my teeth, but am ten pounds heavier than all of my friends. I'm athletic and strong, but I weigh myself daily. I stop eating lunch.

I am self-conscious and uncomfortable in my own skin.

I'm eighteen, and I've graduated at the very top of my class. I have countless scholarships, and am excited to be college-bound. I'm toned and nothing jiggles when I run, but I'm still ten pounds heavier than most of my friends.

My father died over the summer, and I am lost when I leave for college. I still don't eat lunch, and I work out on campus once or twice a day. I'm no longer ten pounds heavier than my friends, and I go out almost every night trying to fill a void that I don't understand. One night, I sink into my bed and cry.

I'm self-conscious and uncomfortable in my own skin.

I'm twenty, and my mom is dying. I leave school to be with her and work part-time. I take diet pills, rarely eat, and am finally thin. I feel proud when people comment on my bony hips.

I'm still self-conscious and uncomfortable in my own skin.

I'm twenty-one, and back in school, without parents, and trying to stay busy. I'm still taking diet pills and working out as frequently as possible. With my work and school schedule, sometimes I forget to eat at all. I'm skinny.

I'm still self-conscious and uncomfortable in my own skin.

I'm twenty-four, out of college, married with a son and a brand new baby girl. I haven't owned a scale in years, and despite the pregnancy changes to my body...

I'm learning, even being self-conscious, to be comfortable in my own skin

Once upon a time, when I was very young, someone told me I was fat. I don't remember when, or where, or who. But that tiny, three-letter word was seared into my psyche at a very young age, permanently altering the way I viewed myself, my body, and how I fit into the world. It would creep in at the most inopportune times, like when it was date night, or an important party.

In my house there are two "F" words, and fat is the worst one. I work hard to maintain a positive body image and be comfortable in my skin, because little eyes are watching all the time.

I've always been fiercely protective of my daughter's body image for this reason. The "F" word still makes me come unglued, and I have no problem letting someone know it. If for

21

no other reason, my years of continued self-loathing have now made me diligent in helping my daughter and other women with self-worth.

Now, I'm in my late thirties, and I often hate everything about the number I see on the scale. The difference is I know that I am no longer defined by that number.

Sometimes, I still feel self-conscious...

But I am absolutely, finally, comfortable in my own skin.

All the Broken Paths

Yvette Whittington

I reflect and think to myself if this was the path I envisioned my life would take. As we grow, our vision changes and grows also. We realize the dreams we had in our twenties is much different than the ones from our thirties, as is true with each milestone we pass. A single moment can change the course of your life. My moment occurred in my twenties.

My twenties were a mixture of so many things. It was frightening, it was also the most fulfilling and the most heartbreaking. If I say I regret my twenties that would imply I regret my beautiful daughters, and I most certainly do not. They were my fulfillment and my joy; they were the only thing that got me through most days. They filled my heart with so much pride at a time when I no longer had any. Everything good in me was because of those two little girls. My twenties also brought about the most profound sense of loss I have ever felt. The loss of my father, watching the strongest man I know become weak and frail, a shell of the strong man I knew. I felt completely helpless, there was nothing I could have done, and the outcome was inevitable. I can remember screaming in my car.

Watching someone you love slowly die a painful death changes you. I can't imagine what must have been going through his mind, when given an expiration date on his life. How can one even grasp the finality of that? How long? Days, weeks, or months? No one knew. What you do know is you will no longer be here for things you always dreamed of. You know for certain within a year your chair will be vacant, you know you will not be able to walk your daughters down the aisle, watch your son marry, meet all the grandchildren, and great grandchildren yet to come. Did he wonder if his children would keep his memory alive? Did he wonder if he would be missed? It has been almost twenty-two years. I sometimes forget the sound of his voice, or the wonderful smile he had. I can't rely on my memory anymore anyway, it has become so foggy. I look at old pictures trying to remember things that were tucked away for safe keeping, but it seems they have abandoned me. I don't know if I am subconsciously blocking them or they are gone forever. I just wish I had more of them to hold on to. His death brought so many different emotions, sadness being the biggest. After his passing, before the crowd of people arrived, I remember sitting on the steps of his house feeling so alone. My father was my protector, the one man I knew who loved me beyond measure. In that moment, I came to the realization I couldn't live the way I was living any longer, and I made a decision to remove myself from difficult circumstances I never asked to be in.

So many people came. Everyone who knew my dad loved him. Not one person had a bad thing to say about him. He was a gentle giant, quick-witted, but still no one would ever know how truly tortured he was within.

A good man with a relentless mind. I can imagine how he felt, I feel it as well. With mental illness, you seldom feel at home anywhere or with anyone. You question your sanity often, your mind races and your heart struggles to keep up with it. You seldom feel contentment. You talk to hide the uncomfortable feeling you get in crowds. And the sadness, this overwhelming sense of worthlessness, you tuck deeper and deeper inside of you.

In the days and weeks that followed, I didn't cry. I silently mourned. Have you ever needed to cry and just couldn't? That was where I was stuck. I hadn't shed a tear. It was as if God knew that once they started they would never stop. I became so numb to the world around me, and I felt as if I was floating through each day in a blur.

I finally chose the day and I was ready, even with all the doubts and questions on if I, alone, would be able to provide for my daughters financially or if I could make it at all. Only, I knew staying was no longer an option. When the day arrived, I packed only our clothes and walked away, and the moment my car pulled out the drive, I knew I had made the right choice.

Still scared and unsure of what the road ahead of me held, I still knew it was better than what I was leaving behind. I looked in my rearview mirror at my daughters in their car seats. They were unaware of how much their little lives were about to change. We made our way to my mom's house. Over the next several weeks I noticed neither of the girls were upset about leaving the life we had, which worried me. That meant that no matter how much I had tried to shield them from the chaos, they were still aware of it, and that made me so sad.

My mom walked in on me crying one day. She asked what was wrong, and I told her that I was embarrassed that I was back at home trying to put the pieces of my shattered life back together. She understood. Weeks passed, then two months passed, and I realized I needed to be on my own. I needed to know I could make it by myself. I found us a little one bedroom apartment. Not only was it little, it was nearly unliveable. But it's what I could afford at that time.

It wasn't easy, barely making ends meet. I spent many nights lying awake wondering if I could really do it. Still, I never contemplated going back.

I turned thirty in that little rundown apartment, and that hit me hard. I eventually found us a much better place to live, lots of room upstairs and downstairs, the rent was steep, but I thought I could handle it. I was wrong. It didn't take long for me to realize it just wasn't possible. With daycare expenses being so high, as well as a higher electricity bill, I had to admit defeat. My family was gracious enough to let me move into my grandparents' home. No one was living there, and it had been vacant for some time. It was a blessing. God's grace surrounded me in those years, there was never a need for long. He always provided.

I had grown, and my vision of my life changed dramatically. We realize the vision we had in our twenties is much different than the reality of our thirties.

I was doing all I could to make it. It seemed as if my daughters were getting sick every week, so that caused me to miss work. My supervisor at the time was pushing me to my limits. And one day I had enough. I remember packing up my things, looking at my co-worker, one who had helped me emotionally during the hardest parts, and saying to her, "I quit. You can tell them when they return."

As I made my way home, all I could think was, *what did I just do? I have two kids at home to feed.* But again I knew leaving was the right decision, even if I handled the decision poorly. It took me two weeks to find a job, the job I maintain to this day.

I befriended a co-worker. It didn't take long for us to share intimate stories of our lives with one another. We were both single parents just trying to make it. I thought falling in love was the last thing on my mind, and even further from his.

It was a specific moment, one I recall clearly. I went from just friendly feelings for this man to being in love with him. I don't know what sparked it, but it was so strong, so true, and so unfamiliar. I had to tell him, I needed him to know what I was feeling.

It didn't go over well. We both tried several times over the following years to make it work. I wanted more; he wanted to take it slow. We both knew we loved each other, but the odds always seemed to be stacked against us.

The insecurities of being unwanted and unloved from my previous, abusive relationship took control. You think once you leave an abusive situation, that you will leave everything with it behind you. But the truth is, you carry it around like a stone. You learn that one way or another, until you accept and come to terms with it, it follows you through each season of your life. I hadn't yet come to terms with mine. I made a decision to take another job at one of our other locations. I knew it was best.

Soon, I learned he had moved on and was dating someone else. It was final. Over.

I found myself in my forties, alone, heartbroken, and working three jobs to make ends meet. However, that path became a time of awakening, a rebirth for me. I stood in my mother's kitchen one day and realized she was my best friend and my biggest, most faithful cheerleader. She had always been there, celebrating my victories, and lending her knowledge and compassion in the times I failed miserably. She was that mother, the one on her knees, and there in her kitchen that day, her words rang truer than they ever had: God was what I ultimately needed.[2]

Adjusting to a new job with people I didn't know took time, the first several months I cried every day as I drove home. I cried because the job was hard, and I had little-to-no guidance. But I mostly cried because I missed him so much. I changed my habits and didn't travel to the small town he lived in for fear of running into him. I knew if I were to see him it would only set me back. A love that strong had the potential to break me for the rest of my life. Lee was my soulmate, the missing piece of my heart, and I knew it.

I decided it was time to find out why I was the way I was. My first appointment with a psychiatrist I shared the racing thoughts, the sadness, and the relentless self-doubt in my mind that drove every bad decision I made. The diagnosis, although quite scary and embarrassing, made sense to me. Finally, after years and years of feeling less capable of controlling my emotions than other people, I finally knew why.

I am my father's child. Even saying Bipolar makes people look at you differently. They often envision a screaming maniac running through the streets wreaking havoc, but that stigma is far from the truth of it. I soon found I was "that" person who has to take medication to be normal, whatever normal is. I was able to finally see stability after being on the medication a few weeks; I felt at peace. I felt a calm I don't think I had ever felt in my life. I started accepting things that I hadn't, like my harmful past and then my lost love. I started praying for Lee, my soulmate. I prayed he was safe and happy. I tried dating and soon realized it just wasn't the right path for me and wasted no time in letting that go. I was no longer timid and passive like I always had been. I had accepted the fact that I would never get married, if I couldn't marry

Lee. After a year of no contact with him at all, I was asked to go pick something up from his location. I suggested someone else go, but there was no one else available. As I made my way there, I could feel the tears in my eyes and my stomach turning flips. I walked in very cautiously, hoping to be in and out quickly and not have to face him. When I saw him and my first instinct was to grab what I came for and leave, I instead decided to go say hello. After all, this was the man I prayed for every day. We talked for a brief moment, and then it was time for me to go. I remember looking at him seeing everything I ever wanted in a man, knowing my wants would never be realized, and I cried all the way back to work.

The next day, I got an email from him. Then an invitation to lunch. It happened very quickly, looking back. My mind was in a quiet place, I was able to accept whatever was happening for what it was and let it happen without questioning exactly what "that" was.

I am now in the first year of my fifties. My forties brought about courage, strength, and unconditional friendship and love. I have had other, much missed, friendships restored. Those women and I are in contact nearly every day. We have our Saturday morning coffee, and our dinner dates, but most importantly we know if one of us needs us, we will drop it all to be there. One of my closest friends tragically almost lost her son recently. I remember coming to the realization that I don't always need to be there physically, but I can text and call, let her know she isn't alone. You would be surprised how a few words of encouragement can restore someone's faith or just empower them to push through in days of uncertainty.

And last, but not least, I can say with great joy that I am happily married to Lee, that soulmate I prayed for through the years. The road to get here wasn't always easy, because I had a lot of roads to travel in my own self-discovery. As did he.

Together, we have our wonderful children, their spouses, and all of our beautiful grandchildren. I did not think this is how my life would've play out. Yet it is so much greater then even I, the bipolar wife, could've ever imagined.

God does things in His time, and His time is always the right time. So whatever visions are in store for me in fifties, I say, bring it on.

Only God knows where the broken paths will take us.

2. Isaiah 41:10

A Seat at the Table

Marcie Klock

My parents divorced when I was young. Mom moved my brother and me away from our dad and the majority of our family—all whom were very vital beings in our childhood. We left the small town of Wise, Virginia to head to the big city in Fredericksburg, which felt much larger to me, because I had come from such a small town. We initially lived with our Uncle Charles, Aunt Glenna, and their kids, my cousins, that became much like my own sister and brothers. The living situation was temporary, until my mom could find a job to save up money for a place of our own, which took a year or so. This living situation quickly became a fundamental time in my life. My family became larger.

For the first time in my life I had structure.

My aunt and uncle were devoted Christians. They had rules, they were strict and disciplined, and they gave an enormous amount of love. They re-arranged their entire house to make room for us to stay with them.[3] Now that I am an adult, I realize lifting and shifting a large family around is not an easy task. I thank God that they made room for us without hesitation.

Family dinners started with prayer. The table was large and no one got up until everyone was finished with their meal, family game night, family discussions, family events. I loved this— every aspect of this, I loved! Not to mention that sitting at the table for those family meals, or just sitting as the gathering place to talk, made me feel important, special, and included, because for most of my life, I only sat at the table with Nana and Wo.

Fast forward to when we left and moved out of my aunt and uncle's and into the city. One evening, my mom was working, and I was home alone. If I ever left the house when she was working and I was alone, her rule was I had to always call to ask her permission before leaving for anything. This particular evening, I was bored and wanted to walk outside along the street in the city. I made the call, and I was given permission to walk to the end of the street and back. It was not a long street, so my walk was pretty limited, but I was happy Mom said yes.

As I was walking, I noticed in one of the houses, there was a family eating dinner. You could easily see into their formal dining room, located at the front of the house. The feeling that instantly came over was me was how much I missed the family dinners and gatherings with my aunt and uncle.

I wanted to be back at the table.

When I approached the next house from the street, again, I could see into the dining area and it was the same thing. I realized then that I was venturing on my walk at dinnertime. When I returned home, I proceeded to make my own dinner and sat alone. It felt odd and deeply lonely to do this at nine years old, but it was what I had to do because my mom had to work and my older brother was hanging out with friends that night.

Years of my childhood passed, and my entire life and world would change when I met my best friend—who is now my husband.

I spent years meeting Jim at coffee shops, talking, and writing back and forth with him. We would spend countless hours talking about his family, but mainly he talked about his because I never really shared a tremendous amount of tradition about my family. He would tell me stories about his family traditions, and I would sit and get lost at his stories of gatherings, all around their table.

I longed to be at that table again.

His family seemed almost identical to my Uncle Charles and Aunt Glenna. Over the years, I would often have visions of myself with Jim at his family gatherings. I imagined it would be a lot like my aunt and uncle's, and Nana and Wo's, and those families I saw from the street in Fredericksburg that day my Mom allowed me to go on that walk. Because my husband and I had a friendship that spanned for many years prior to getting married, it would be a long time before I would get the opportunity to be with him at his family gatherings. I often dreamed of it though, because his discussions would take me back to the one year in my childhood where there was love, faith, stability, family games, fun, laughter, and structure.

My husband has a younger brother, Rossie,

who is autistic. He's been the biggest blessing that I have gained through my husband's family. I don't get to see him often, but I love him with my whole heart. His face and presence make me feel this abundance of love as soon as he enters any room. Rossie's schedule is not like ours. He has his own routine. Sometimes, he sleeps during the day. When he wakes up, the first thing he does is walk upstairs from his bedroom and come to the table in the kitchen. He often stands. He usually does not sit at the table. He talks, smiles, loves, and walks away when he's ready. Sometimes, he is there for a short time, and sometimes he stays awhile. There is something about Rossie that makes me feel this overwhelming amount of joy when he comes to the table.

Jim also has five sisters—two older, and two younger, and one older sister that passed away. During our pre-marriage conversations through the years, I imagined myself being a sister too. I simply thought, and dreamed, that one day I would marry this man, have my seat at the table, have sisters, a momma, and daddy—much like that time in my life I often think of.

Recently, while out with one of my dearest sister-friends, Lindsey, I explained some of this story to her. I mainly emphasized the table, the significance and what it meant to me to feel loved, included, and a part of a family—to never again be on the outside. I talked about the families that have loved me and invited me to their table. That experience did not happen with my birth mother and father. That came to me from other people that loved me like a mother and father do. I will be forever grateful to them for this. Lindsey and I had some time to kill before seeing a movie, so we decided to have cocktails while we waited. When we sat at a window-front table, I looked over to finish my conversation, and she was looking at me with a half-smile.

"I think you are learning to make a table with your own family," she nudged me, "Sis, we are at the table."

Jim and I have been married for years now, and sitting at the family table hasn't been as easy as I dreamed or often imagined. For a good portion of our marriage, we've had to live apart at times as our careers have us in different locations. It's by no means traditional, but we are blessed in making it work well. I have come to realize that sometimes our hopes, dreams, and wishes sometimes don't turn out the way we plan.[4]

You see, I learned that it doesn't have to be people with a blood bond or same last name as you that can give you *your* seat at the table.

And also that you could be someone else's seat.

3. Hebrews 13:16
4. Proverbs 16:9

Don't Wait

Sherry Reamer

There are many things in life that we should wait for: a ride to work, a new baby to arrive, a party to attend, and so on. But some things in life should be done or said whenever the Lord moves you to do so. This is my story of how the Lord told me to do something important, and I did it, but only halfway.

At times during my adult life, the Lord has awakened me in the middle of the night and moved me to write. Sometimes it was a poem, sometimes just a paragraph, and occasionally a short story. One time the Lord revealed to me in a dream that I should make up with my mom as soon as possible, after an argument that we'd had. In the dream, Mother and I weren't speaking for some insignificant reason, and before I could try to resolve our differences, she died. In the dream, I was left crying beside her grave, wishing that I could have her back for just five minutes so that I could hold her and tell her how much I loved her—to say that I was sorry for the things I had said to her. The next day I called her on the phone and told her that I was so sorry for being short with her and asked her to forgive me. She did so happily, and we never had another argument for the rest of our lives.

Years later, the Lord awakened me again from a dream, one that I know without a doubt was orchestrated by Him. In the dream, He told me to awaken and write a letter to my brother as though it was written by my mother's hand, and then I should give it to him straight away. In it I should tell him how much she loved him, how proud of him she had always been, and to ask him to forgive her for anything she had done to hurt him when he was young. I had known for a while that my brother held on to some memories that were painful to him regarding our mom, and I knew that the Lord had me write this letter as a way of helping him find closure for that part of his life. Again, remember that God instructed me to write the letter in my mother's stead. And so I awoke from the dream and wrote the letter just as He instructed. But unlike in my dream, I didn't give the letter to him as I was told to do. I remember thinking, okay the next time I see him I'm going to give it to him. But I didn't see him every day, or even every week, so I packed it around in my purse with the intent of giving it to him, eventually. The longer I waited to give the letter to him, the more anxious I became thinking he may get angry with me for writing it, or that he may think I was foolish. So one day I just moved it from my purse to the glove compartment in my car, and there it sat for months.

Unbeknown to me, God was working in my brother's life and preparing him for what was to come next. You see, Mother's health had been deteriorating for a while, and the family could no longer take care of her. She was taken to a nursing home where she lived the last year and a half of her life. When her time was near, we took turns going to her room and sitting with her. At some point prior to this time, my brother must have forgiven her, because he would sit for hours with her, holding her hand and praying. She was not conscious at that time, but I believe she knew he was there.

Mother passed away quietly and without pain. She had expressed to the family that she didn't want to be on any type of life support; she was ready to go when God called her home. It was difficult to watch her health decline, but we fulfilled her wish. And still, the letter to my brother stayed in the glove compartment of my car.

Then, one afternoon exactly two months and two days after Mother died, I had gotten off work and headed to the beauty salon. While on the way, I received a phone call from my husband, telling me that my brother had been taken to the emergency room. I began to cry profusely, turned my car around and headed to the hospital. Little did I know the urgency with which I drove to the hospital was not needed, because my brother lay dead, his body lifeless on a gurney in the emergency room. I remember walking into the room expecting to see him being tended to by doctors and nurses, but I was completely unprepared for what I saw. I felt as though I was suddenly surrounded by a fog—a fog that choked the very breath from me and caused my knees to buckle. I remember reaching out to touch his hands, the hands that were so masculine in life and always doing things to help others in need. He was always helping family members, friends, and even perfect strangers in one way or another. His work ethic was above reproach. Everyone that knew him, knew that when he told you something, it would be the absolute truth. The hands that I now held were cold and swollen in death, along with the rest of his body. Disbelief clouded my mind as I struggled to comprehend that he was no longer with us. At some point, I remember running from the room, out of the hospital doors, and collapsing on the ramp outside. Before I realized it, I had begun to wail like I had never done in my entire life. I felt as though something or someone had ripped out my heart. I kept thinking, *why did I not give him the letter that God had instructed me to write and give to him?* The guilt I felt for not completing the task the Lord had given me, and losing my brother all at the same time, was devastating.

Eventually, I managed to walk back into the hospital room where he lay. The family stood around his bed, still not comprehending that he was gone. Someone said he had suffered a heart attack. No autopsy was performed, but

45

based on the symptoms he had just prior to his death, it did appear he had a heart attack. His daughter was studying to be a nurse at the time and happened to be there when he collapsed. She performed CPR on him, but he did not respond. I can't begin to imagine how she must have felt that day and in the days to come, trying her best to save him, but to no avail. I now know that the Lord called him home, to give him the rest he so richly deserved.

On the day of his funeral, I stood looking down at him lying in his coffin, knowing that I could have made a difference for him by giving him the letter God had instructed me to write.

Oh how I cried and wished that I had done what He told me to do, but it was too late. So with the letter in my hand, I leaned down to tell him goodbye one last time, and tucked the envelope in the breast pocket of his suit coat. I sobbed and told him that I loved him, begged him to forgive me for not giving him the letter, and then returned to the pew. I vaguely remember the music that was sung, and those who stood to give testament to the wonderful man that my brother was. I even remember the pastor saying words of encouragement from the Bible. But mostly, I remember the guilt and shame I felt for not having done what God commanded me to do.

In the days that followed, my sister and I struggled to make sense of his untimely death. As for myself, I felt as though there was a hole in the middle of my chest, near my heart. This hole could not be filled. The pain I experienced could not be alleviated, no matter how much I prayed and tried to work things out in my heart and mind.

Fortunately, our sister-in-law recommended a program for us to attend at a nearby church. The program was Christian-based to help people recover from different types of addictions, but was also for those affected by their loved one's problems. The program did not include a grief recovery class, but we weren't aware of that at the time and proceeded to sit in on a meeting. Even though we weren't sure that we were in the right place, something told both of us to give it a try. We went into one of the women's classes that we thought would best fit our situation. Even though no one in the class was there due to the loss of a loved one, we were eventually comfortable enough to share our loss with the group. We even began attending small group classes at one of the lady's homes, working through our grief, as well as others problems we realized were also in our hearts.

Over the next year, we attended the program and classes at the church on Friday nights, and the small group classes at someone's home on Wednesdays. My sister and I grew closer to the Lord, the ladies in our group, and each other. After one year had passed, we both felt that we no longer needed the program ourselves. She stopped going, but I felt moved to stay another year and give back to the program. I was asked to co-lead a group, which I gladly accepted. It was an experience for which I am deeply grateful.

Time, prayer, and trying to get on with life can help heal the loss of a loved one, but grief coupled with guilt is even harder. Knowing that you cannot go back and undo something you said or did, or should have said or done eats at you like a cancer and can eventually cause physical, mental, and spiritual problems.

If there are things in your life that you need to do, especially if you know the Lord is telling you to do them, *don't wait.* A better time may never present itself. Try to right a wrong that you may have done, whether intentional or not. Forgive someone who may have harmed you in some way. Tell that person who means so much to you, that you love them and cherish them. Don't go one more day without doing or saying what you know is the right thing. Make amends where you can before it is too late, and your life and the lives of others will be better for it. The Lord will bless you for it in ways that you cannot begin to imagine.

Just don't wait!

Conflict Mode

Michelle Jester

One of the greatest barriers we face in relationships is the problem of communication, especially in confrontation. When someone I love and trust confronts me, I am learning to stop and listen. It's hard, because I know I never intend to hurt someone close to me. I want to quickly alleviate that issue first, rather than address the other person's issue. I always felt that if I helped them realize I would never have hurt them on purpose, the issue would've been resolved and there would've been no need to discuss it any further. However, I'm realizing that in them coming to me to address their issue, they are likely already close enough to me to know my intent.

And that good intention does not dispel a problem.

My children told me that I am not one to back down, which I already knew, but here is the worst part ... so it makes it difficult for others to confront me. Of course I waved off this statement, because it was silly. *I am the easiest person to talk to,* I thought. I'm not someone who screams and shouts. I'm fairly level-headed and confident. I try to be understanding and full of grace.

But I am realizing more and more those traits are only at the forefront when I am helping others with problems that don't have to do *with* me.

I am the *confronter.* Not to be confused with the instigator, because I am only talking about in a reactionary situation. When a conflict arises, I confront it. And from what my children have said, I confront it full-on. Unfortunately, since I don't have any problems with confronting a problem, and I want to get my intentions out of the way first, it makes some people stop communicating at some point, or not want to confront an issue with me at all.

And that is a problem. One I am working on.

I'm focusing on the reaction, less than the emotion, because we all have feelings; we all get hurt and angry. I obviously don't want for someone to think I hurt them on purpose, and I certainly can't own a hurt that had nothing to do with me. But hurt is real, and it's in how we let that hurt manifest in our actions that matter to our communication with others.

With many daughters, my own included, communication is difficult sometimes, because their hurt can have many variables. I may have said something I'd said fifty times throughout their life, but on a day where others have hurt them, or they are dealing with other issues, that statement may truly wound them. Or maybe because they'd already been hurt by others it made it easier for them to tell me something upset them, that they'd never shared before. But ... and a big but ... because we have to work harder at problem resolution, we also have stronger relationships.

I'm no expert, however through the years I've started to analyze my relationships more and have come to the conclusion that there are several types of personalities when it comes to resolving relationship issues. I've already revealed that I am the confronter. A positive about the confronter is that they also confront themselves. And after they deal with issues, say what needs to be said, they move on.

One of my best friends, whom I love dearly, is the *runner*. She called one day about an issue she was having with another friend and I said, "Don't run." She sat on the phone for a few seconds absorbing that and then replied, "Wow, yes. I do want to run." To which I replied, "Yes, and I always confront, when I should sometimes take a break first." She laughed and agreed wholeheartedly. We communicate better than we ever have after acknowledging that about each other. A positive aspect about runners is that they typically do return and face the issue until it is fully addressed. A negative is, it won't be on your timeline. If you're a confronter, you'll have to decide if the relationship is worth the patience and effort. However, if you can let them run, wait until they are ready; they will get their own clarity and return to work through the conflict.

Another one of my close friends is the *appeaser,* or *avoider*. It doesn't matter what it's about, she just avoids all conflict, even to her own detriment, by agreeing. If anyone tries to address something with her, she simply agrees,

"Yeah, I get that," or "True," or "Maybe." The appeaser/avoider doesn't want to talk about it, so they simply agree in an attempt to avoid any further discussions. A positive of this type, is they usually face the problem internally and try to weigh if it is something they need to change. A negative is they will more often than not, never tell you about it, and your actual conflict may never be resolved through back-and-forth communication. The good news about this type is they heavily consider the issue. If they find they need to change, they will, and typically not repeat the offense.

Another type is the *ignorer*. We all have at least one of these in our lives. No matter what you address, from them parking in the wrong space every single time they come to the office, to them leaving you hanging by not showing up to a planned lunch date, they will ignore you. This can seem like the avoider on many levels, but look deeper and there are very strong differences. The main one is ignorers simply won't hear out any of your issues and refuse to internally address any of the actions that caused them; hence they repeat it over and over. What can seem like a positive about ignorers, that they also ignore your faults in return, is actually another negative. It can be difficult to have an honest, deeper relationship with them, which causes it to stay on a superficial level. The encouraging news about this type however, is that in given time, if you are willing to put in the work, they can learn that you will love them even when you have a problem with them, and communication can start to open.

Finally, the *blocker*. No matter how big or how small an issue is, they immediately block whatever you are trying to address by getting angry or stopping the conversation altogether. They don't want to talk or discuss, and will make every confrontation turn negative. Blockers block all talk no matter what, and they are stubborn. A positive is that blockers tend to assess issues on their own, tend to face the issue if you condense it to a sentence or two, and not drag it out over a full-hour conversation. A negative is that they typically think changes only occur through their self-reflection, and not through conflict resolution, so they may never accept that you brought an issue to them. Still, if you can handle not getting the credit, you'll get the result of better future conflict communication.

I think it really boils down to insecurities, which we all have. If we can value the insecurities in others, and realize we possess them also, we can improve the overall value of each of our worth.

It may seem difficult to understand how we can better communicate with others, but ultimately we all desire the same things: better relationships, better communication, and overall wellness.

And keep in mind, getting a "sorry" or having your feelings validated may seem like the solution, but they really aren't. Those only make you feel temporarily satisfied, until the next time an issue arises.

I'm starting by evaluating my own way of reacting to conflict. I know I can't truly change another person or their reactions, however, I can begin by acknowledging my own actions, and understanding how others deal with issues, making a way for better communication with the people I care for.

From the Ruin

Tiara Purnell

Saying that our lives have all changed dramatically in recent times, is an understatement. The world seemed like a train coming to its next stop, and it has yet to pick up full-steam. It's monotonous, yet scary.

Many women seem to be thinking, and overthinking, about our next crisis or our next reward. One thing is for certain, it is the time to think about your financial position in the world. If you weren't already ahead of the curve, you are finding yourself behind it. The pandemic snatched many of us from a state of busyness, but also from our business. However, out of this situation we can find what happens when preparation and opportunity meet.

I can tell you it can be the recipe to financial success.

While you may feel it's impossible, it is still fact that this is a perfect season for growth and building financial independence.

You have to choose to make an alignment between your calling, your passion, or your dream. We so often underestimate the power of God's timing, I've done it also. Think about the power of a total eclipse—the sun, moon, and earth aligning. While most folks are in awe, because it is majestic, some are simply left in darkness. There is a shift. We have to trust God with all things that include time and money.

These two things go hand-in-hand.

In a time where we've all slimmed down our spending and learned what we really need to survive and thrive, it is an opportunity for change—for a new aligning.

Start a business!

Go for the promotion!

Seize the opportunity to be in alignment with what you spend your time and money on. [5]

Start the business of your dreams.

If your job does not value skills that you have mastered, think of starting a business, or in modern-day vernacular, a side hustle! To start a business is fairly easy—a retail business or a consulting business. From making candles, to designing apparel, to teaching a skill or tutoring online.

We all have gift.

Don't underestimate yourself and where God can bring you. The platform options are limitless for an online business. There is Squarespace, Esty, Shopify, Volusion, etc. A few clicks and you're done. Teach a skill or a craft through various platforms such as Udemy, Teachable, and Thinkific. You have a talent, now all you have to do is make it available on social media platforms and sell it.[6]

Go for that promotion.

During the stay-at-home order, time and thought was of the essence. You may have felt hopeless about your job and also about the day of returning to it. You may have realized there was a sense of repetitiveness and a cycle with no end at your job. You may have started to question yourself: *Is this the job for me?*

One of the most important questions you should be asking now is: *What was I was called to do?*

Years ago, I found myself asking that question, and I realigned. It's not always easy, but it's always worth it.

If you have a dream, in those feelings, you have to channel the energy to change. Now is the time. Go back to your vision-board. There is a dream job pinned there. Create a plan of action to get to the next destination. You can do this!

The first step is the step of faith.

Find the place that makes you happy. We are fearfully and wonderfully made with gifts and talents. We each fit a part. With God, and his guidance and promises, we can find our way there.

React to the calling, dream, or passion that has been given to you by God, and in that you'll find your life.

5. Ecclesiastes 3:1
6. Exodus 31:3-5

Dear Future Me

Karen K. Scott

Recently I read this quote:

"If you are depressed,
you're living in the PAST.
If you are anxious,
you are living in the FUTURE.
If you are at peace,
you are living in the PRESENT."
–Lao Tzu

It promtped me to write the following letter.

Dear Future Me,

If you find yourself living in all three of these: past, future, and present, at the same time, give yourself a break.

At night when your mind is continuously going, you may feel anxiety for no reason, you may also feel secluded. I would like for you to go and hang with friends. I know, "Why, when I can lie on the sofa, sleep, and watch TV?" However, if you do get out, maybe go to a family function, work event, or concert. You may find that you will feel better. You will likely smile and enjoy yourself.[7] (Until yourself tells you it is time to go, that is. Then go. Know your limitations.)

I want you to want change, seek change, actively work at the change, and finally embrace change.

Depression, anxiety, PTSD, and other mental issues plague so many of us, and I don't want you to overlook it. Those symptoms don't often simply go away. They must be faced, walked through, and accepted.

Change is difficult.

It is uncomfortable.

However, it is progression. The world is ever-changing and so are we.

Find people who encourage you and speak good things over your life.[8]

Finally, know that you can't change the past, and

you may never see the future.

So, live in the present.

Love life, work towards personal development, and do simple things that make you happy. Fall in love with them and yourself all over again.

Love,

Me

> "If you can change your mind,
> you can change your life."
> –William James

7. Proverbs 17:22
8. Proverbs 12:25

Letting Love Find Me

Aimee Bennett

At twenty-five years old, I had already lost my mom and a best friend. I was divorced and a single mom of a four-year-old. Those events rocked my already shaky faith in God. I believed in a higher power, whatever that was. I believed in destiny and that things worked out how they were supposed to, but ultimately my faith in a god was diminishing.

My mom had always told me, "What's meant to be, will always find a way." As a teenager and young adult, I hated when she said those words to me, but I believed them. However, at twenty-five, I found it nearly impossible to be at peace with the worries that consumed my life. Don't get me wrong, I loved my life on the surface. I had friends, a social life, and a job that allowed me to do whatever I needed for my son. I had even bought a house that summer, by myself.

My life looked like what a lot of other women told me they'd wished theirs was.

I was one of the most independent females I knew, but I was also lonely. I wanted more. I wanted stability and a love that would withstand whatever the world threw at it. I desired to know someone, and them to know me so intimately that we felt like we were one. Someone who, instead of battling each other, would battle the world with me.

When my first marriage ended, I felt like a failure. Society definitely doesn't look at divorce in a good light, so I was also a failure to the world. Every time I had to say, "Oh … no, we're divorced," I fell further and further into the pit of failure. To others, it never matters why a marriage didn't work out, only that it didn't.

I worried that I would never have that someone to share my home with, and I longed for it. I wanted companionship and to have another child. I'd always hoped my kids could have a small age gap between them, so they would remain close. Ultimately, I wanted what my grandparents had—a beautiful, sixty-year marriage.

Looking back now, it seems I never went for the men who may have actually liked me; I was left being rejected by the ones I really thought I liked.

With my second marriage, I hadn't seen any red flags with how fast it all happened, because I was completely in love. We started dating, soon were head-over-heels, and decided to get married only a few months later.

Immediately after marrying, major problems started cropping up. Friends I'd known for years, men and women, were no longer approved of by my husband. I couldn't meet up with my girlfriends anymore, like I always had. My independence, that had initially attracted him, suddenly became our biggest issue. I felt more and more like nothing that I gave up would ever be enough. I had tried changing and doing the things I thought I should, but nothing was righted in our relationship as a result, and I was miserable. Soon our marriage began to run on autopilot.

I began working as a secretary at a local church just after our wedding. It was a running joke that no one could believe I hadn't burst into flames just by walking through the door. After a few months, I decided to take a leap of faith by visiting on Sundays.

That's when God got me.

Shortly after my daughter was born, I slowly started to learn about God's love and witnessed people who genuinely cared for me. The people of that church were gracious and loving. I felt accepted and valuable. I became actively involved and over the following years, my faith and relationship with God grew tremendously. While I was growing in God, my marriage was crumbling, because it only added more insecurity for my husband.

When we later bought my grandparents' house, it needed to be updated. We both felt that being there, living in the house that inspired my own desires of commitment and longevity in a relationship, would somehow mend what was broken between us. However, life was already stressful with kids and work. Adding a second mortgage before our other house was sold made the problems between us exponentially worse. I dove into my kids' lives and busied myself with home improvements; he dove into his work.

I was at a point where all I wanted was for us to both be happy, and more and more it became evident that it would never happen while we were together.

Still, the last thing I wanted was to get a divorce. Again.

I didn't want to give up or fail. I already had to share custody of my son. I didn't want my daughter to come from a "broken" home, too. It's sad that children are still judged by divorce. I've always found that odd. Though, going through it this time, I am starting to understand it somewhat. What had the children seen through the broken marriage? What had they been through? How will it affect them moving forward?

All solid concerns.

I have an amicable relationship with my son's father, and we continue to work on it for our son. The best I can hope for is to one day have that with my second husband.

At thirty-four years old, I'm again a single mom. However, this time around I have my faith. I've done a lot of praying, my fair share of crying, and spent more time being angry than I like to admit. I know though, without a doubt, that God will bring me through this season.

I still desire the connection my grandparents had. I desire to find the person who I will grow old with, love with, and laugh with. Someone stable, to build a love that will withstand whatever the world throws at it.

God will not let me fail, and He will heal my wounds.

I find overwhelming comfort in knowing that God has someone out there for me.

Someone who I know and knows me so intimately that we are one. This time around, I am in no hurry. When God knows I am ready, He will send who He wants for me into my life. I look forward to living the life God has planned for me until then.

With all that I've been through, I am finally becoming the person God wants me to be. ... and that person is the one who is in love with Him first.

I'm Still Here

Lynn Pallaske

I grew up in house with domestic violence. First with my father, and then my brother. My mother is not someone that anyone would think of as a victim. She is such a strong woman. She's been my hero my whole life, and all I've ever wanted was to be as strong as she is.

That pressure I put on myself was my downfall. I was doing so much my sophomore year in high school and was always busy. On top of that, I got shingles! That should have been a warning, a pause, but I didn't heed it.

All it took was one night.

I trusted my boss, an adult, when I shouldn't have. I thought I was not going to be a statistic, but there I was, sitting in his passenger seat, drunk.

Raped.

The struggle that took over a decade to get through was the fight, flight, and freeze response. I froze, I FROZE! Some people just can't understand the guilt associated with that.

No Sleep Unturned

In the silence
is the torture.
The thoughts
brewing and
stirred appear.
No quiet whispers,
but the rattling
of the mob.
The hush
of the dark
is disturbed
that always
come in
the silence.

It only took a little over a year before I started believing I deserved what he did and what I'd done to myself after. That year was my first suicide attempt and my first visit to the Intensive Care Unit.

I was twenty.

My mother told me that I couldn't leave her; we were supposed to grow old together. That worked for a bit, but nothing really works until you face the truths of your life and all the feelings of inadequacy.

I survived the bottles of medicine I swallowed, like a game, and falling from the top bunk. I didn't feel very alive, though.

I made it through college. Through unwanted comments and touches from prying assumptions.

I survived five years until I woke up in the ICU, again. That time, I knew I was going to fail graduate school. I was just six weeks in, but I was already a failure.

I even failed at killing myself. Just a failure, I failed again.

And again.

The Edge

I fear being at the edge
where you can simply choose
to fly or walk away.

One is more respected
the other less painful,
but I can only choose one.

At the edge there is an end
that can be seen far below.
Behind lays a long hard road.

No one knows where the road leads,
so how does someone choose,
a life that may never see happiness?
Here is a familiar hand to pull me away.

The hand is there to squeeze when scared
and to hold the whole way down the road,
going further from the edge.

Ten long years.

Then, I spent two months in a behavioral health inpatient program. That is when I got to dig deep into my memories, and was finally able to say them out loud. I got to hear what others survived, too.

What I learned was no one's story is worse or better than yours. It's *your* story filled with *your* pain. My pain lives in me like a lifelong friend, and it will not leave me; it's there. But, it is also my strength.

I was a victim for a long time, too long.

Now, I know I'm a survivor, and I am still here.

Here. After all of these years.

I'm sorry for whatever pain you have; something I wish more people would've said to me. My hope is that you realize you are not alone. You are here. You are still here, too.

It is hard work and more pain when the scabs are picked at old wounds, but the cliché is true; it will get better.

You will get better.

I am better.

And I'm still here.

Lotus in Bloom

Keeley Brooks

Three little words have echoed continuously throughout my mind for as long as I can remember. First at my own questioning and second from a psychiatrist. As a child, I knew something was different about me. The way I thought and processed things. The way I felt and understood things. People ... life ... the entire world around me. By the time I reached my early teens, I knew something was not only different, but also wrong.

I was having incessant, frightening

thoughts about the past, present, and future; I was having severe panic attacks that left me shaking uncontrollably, unable to breathe. I was obsessing over suicide. I was devoured with self-image and with what others thought about me. I spent several hours every morning trying to fix or hide everything I hated about myself—things other people or kids made fun of or pointed out to me in public. I couldn't stop comparing myself to everyone else, trying desperately to look like, and be, someone I wasn't.

I couldn't manage my emotions and was stuck in the pit of despair and self-hatred so deeply that I would secretly closed-fist beat myself on an almost-daily basis. And while yes, those things are certainly concerning and surely required professional care, I want to be clear here that those "things" (or their causes, rather) didn't make me wrong, which is exactly what I thought and felt at the time and have for most of my life. Until recently. After nearly thirty years of feeling wrong, I finally got mad enough—so mad, in fact, that without my full awareness, my perspective shifted on its own. But I didn't just get mad; I got angry ... quietly angry ... inherently angry—the worst kind of angry, to be honest. I got so angry, in fact, that I made a conscious, worry-free decision to run full force through the anger and fear and loathing and dive head first into all of the things society and popular culture had labeled as "wrong" with me.

When I was twenty, I was diagnosed with not one, but four, mental illnesses.

Generalized Anxiety Disorder, Panic Disorder, Obsessive-Compulsive Disorder, and Major Clinical Depression. Then, as if those diagnoses weren't enough, a fifth one was identified under a new doctor a short eighteen months later. Borderline Personality Disorder.

For the unfamiliar, BPD is a mental health disorder impacting the way you think and feel, not just about yourself, but about others as well. It causes problems functioning in everyday life, self-image issues, difficulty managing emotions and behavior, and (the kicker!) a pattern of unstable relationships. That was the one that truly scared me, not because of what it meant. It scared me because of what I worried it would mean to and for other people ... the loved ones in my life. And honestly, at the time when I heard, "You have a personality disorder," all I could do was get hung up in the endless cycle of those words. That diagnosis shamed me even further into the ruminating thought that having a personality disorder indeed meant that I am wrong and unworthy. I felt like I needed to hide who I was from those I like to call "the normals." I worried if they would even want to be around me knowing I was so diseased and abnormal. I worried how anyone could ever tolerate or love me, and after too many questions and comments about how difficult I was to be around or what was wrong with me, I buried myself so deeply in shame that I privately, physically beat myself over it for nearly twenty-five years.

It was 2003, and I was so close to graduating LSU with a bachelor's degree when I was diagnosed with BPD. I was struggling to get through classes, but I was still showing up and trying, even if it meant pacing in the hall and talking the active battle lines of my diseases down when they were armed, bloodthirsty, and raging for war. I was struggling to sleep, eat, wake, bathe, dress, leave the house, get to work, be an adult/daughter/sibling/partner, pay bills, be a friend, have friends, write, laugh, love, understand myself—you name it. Then, one day, at my monthly psychiatrist visit, my doctor said, "You know, Keeley, you might want to consider getting on disability. Right now, with all the stress, you're really not mentally fit to take on all the things you're dealing with. I'm going to write you a letter for your classes and your department, and you should take some time off work."

Hold up, I thought. *Not mentally fit? Did I really just hear that?* I did. She'd said I wasn't mentally fit.

What?

I was frozen in shame, overwhelmed at the thought of what others might think and say about me. Like a prisoner in chains, I just sat there, speechless. When I heard that medically I was "not mentally fit" to do something, it shattered and devastated me, or what was left of me. To hear that I should consider disability assistance made me feel relieved on some level to know I could get some support, but more than anything, it just made me feel even worse about myself. How could I do that when there are so many other people in Louisiana with more severe levels of my disabilities, or with even worse disabilities? I felt ashamed on the deepest, darkest levels as those three words splintered into me like a billion tiny shards of glass, leaving the label "not mentally fit" to flow through me like white noise. You know the sound, it's voiceless—tuneless—except it isn't really noise at all. It's this vacant silence so deafening, it drives you mad. I don't mean mad in emotion; I mean Edgar-Allen-Poe mad. And even though you are alone in this silence, you can't escape its vacancy; it follows and hunts you wherever you go, in whatever you do. Sometimes you hear it over the sound of another's voice in conversation. Sometimes you hear it over a crowd of roaring college football fans. Sometimes it even dominates a chorus of screaming cicadas like they were never even there. Other times, though, you hear it in your sleep, and that's the scary part—a diseased reminder to torment you even when you're unconscious. There was no escape, and that was frightening.

These are the games mental illness plays with you. Just like a chorus of fertile, brilliantly singing cicadas, mental illness infiltrates the garden of your mind and lays its eggs on your tiny baby plants of hope, knowing that each separate mental issue will work its darkness to ensure the eggs grow to maturity, ensuring death. And just when all of your hopeful positivity plants die, your mental illnesses manifest and tear through the soil of your mind to begin planting their own seeds—seeds of negativity and fear they water and sow in rituals of pride and power. Sleep seems like your only friend, your one real escape from the sound. But that's a big, fat lie. You don't even realize you still hear it all night long, and you know this because it's your ringing ears and echoing label that irritate, kick up the cycle of terrifying thoughts, and jolt you awake each day. You also don't realize that the only thing preventing you from obsessing over the presence of the sound for a full twenty-four hours a day is your hypnotic state of restless sleep. Then, when you wake, you begin to pray that maybe, just maybe you will be safe from the sound. But as you gain consciousness, so too does the sound. Some days, it is twice as loud and invasive as the day before, almost as though in an act of retribution, your inner self has weakened your ability to fight simply because nature has taken its course and you have fallen asleep.

Now you're severely stuck, rooted in shame so deeply that your mission becomes not to survive and appear normal; it becomes to protect your truth and hide it from everyone around you. You know you simply cannot bear another bit of teasing, another wisecrack about mental illness, or another jab from someone you love simply because they see you as difficult and emotional and wrong. And that's when it gets louder and louder, ensuring that every time you swallow or blink or breathe, all you hear is that deafening echo of the label "not mentally fit."

Not mentally fit.

Not mentally fit.

Not mentally fit.

You remember everything anyone ever said to you over the course of your life about how something is wrong with you. "What is *wrong* with you?" they'd ask in confusion and disgust, but never sincerity.

"I can't stand to be around you when you're like this," they'd say.

"The way you are, Keeley, I'd rather have you as a memory than to have you in my life at all," my own father would say.

It's all you remember over the only thing you can hear: that deafening, echoing sound left behind by a label others provided and then hung over your head. And that becomes enough to frighten you even deeper into the fear and shame that have become a vital part of your being, just as bones and blood and identifying features are.

Now you find yourself making desperate attempts to drown out the sound, but nothing seems to work. Your mind is working overtime, in overdrive, to beat you into submission under that echoing sound that rings on the minute, every minute, every hour, without missing a beat. You close your eyes and start whispering to yourself while covering your ears and trying your best to concentrate on something else— anything other than what you think you are hearing. But it doesn't work. It never goes away no matter how loudly you talk to yourself, how many suggested methods of self-help you engage in, or how much noise you make. It just lingers in the air like thick smoke, eventually becoming a part of you, becoming a necessity to survive in your own world. And when that happens, you know there is nothing you can do, but surrender to it.

You coexist.

This has been my relationship with the label "not mentally fit." It has haunted me. For nearly thirty years, I felt like I was trapped in this body of wrongness and shame and mental unfitness—complete ugliness. Some distant being I could not access. I knew somewhere deep down, the real me was still there. A little bit of her, at least. And when I looked hard enough, I could see her barely peering out through a pair of lifeless, ditch-water brown eyes, almost as though I, the real me, really was still in there.

Being so mentally, physically, emotionally,

and spiritually weak meant easily giving in to the effects of my mental unfitness and surrendering to it every single time. Eventually, my body would throb and bleed as countless thick, opaque streams barreled their way down my face. And when that dam finally broke for me, there was nothing I could do, but let go of those eyelids and surrender to the sea of mental illness and all its monsters churning hungrily inside me.

To my surprise, when I did that, the real discovery of who I truly am, began.

When I let go, I left being "wrong." Did that mean that everything was fixed and happy and all sunshine and snowballs?

Absolutely not.

It meant that when I stopped running from and trying to conceal who I was, that deafening sound, over time, began to decrease. The more I faced my truths, the more I felt my symptoms beginning to relax in my soul. On that level, I felt like I could breathe again. The more I embraced the real me, the less I embraced most of the self-hatred and hurtful comments and actions from others. The more I surrendered to learning about myself and to living that truth in a way that honored my being, my hardened heart began to soften its edges. My perspective on myself, my diseases, life—everything—slowly began to change. Gradually, my days became less about hiding, pretending, and hating, and more about slowing down, listening to and being gentle with myself, and finding ways to better understand and love myself, no matter how painful or difficult it was.

I did the opposite of what I was taught to do and started focusing my perspective inward. I stopped feeding my face with the smorgasbord of psychotropic pills put in front of me just because a doctor said I should take them, despite my reports of increased suicidal thoughts and tendencies. Side effects like that are never okay. I began to educate myself on different healthcare options and started experimenting with subtle changes.

Today I live as best I can in ways that better serve me. I manage my health in more organic ways: a better, cleaner diet full of plants and herbs; meditation, breathing exercises, yoga and martial arts; and animal therapy, music therapy, and art therapy on my own terms, to name a few. By no means are things perfect, but I can breathe easier today than I ever have my whole life.

I have good days and bad, strikes and gutters, ups and downs. We all do. Point is, I accept that. I do the best I can, when I can, how I can, and I give Keeley a break when someone thinks that's not enough or when my differently-wired brain tells me it's not enough. I listen to my body and my spirit for what they need and thusly I need, not to what some cultural, societal, or familial expectation says I need or should be doing. I disconnect from trying to hide and make a mindful, positive effort to connect with who I truly am and present that self in ways that make me feel proud, not others. It has taken time, but I now am careful to surround myself with lovers, not haters, because, let's be honest, who has time for that? I used to have endless time for it. No more ... regardless of who they are.

Surrender is never easy. Mine took thirty years, and it was bloody, deadly, traumatizing, and hurtful. Not just to me, but to those who loved me most, and for that I will remain eternally sorry.

I will not, however, be ashamed.

I will not allow another person and their thoughts, comments, and actions to make me feel ashamed. And I will no longer be ashamed of the mud in my chemical, mental, emotional, or physical makeup. Without that mud, I would not be the person I am today, rooted in bravery and vulnerability in willing to share my truth with the world. I will stand here beaming with strength and courage just like a sweetly blooming lotus flower.

Lotus flowers are my favorite. Not for the way they look, but for the way they grow and what their growth represents. They are breathtakingly beautiful when in bloom ... the shape of each petal so perfectly conformed to hug the pad of your thumb, such a comfortable and organic fit. Its colors encompass the entire rainbow with shades from pink to white to purple to yellow to peach to blue. When closed, they almost look like roses. Beautiful, indeed, but that's not why they're special.

Lotuses grow in wetlands. Louisiana is a wetland; I am Louisiana born and bred.

Lotuses are aquatic plants rooted in mud. I am an aquatic plant rooted in the mud of mental and emotional illness.

Lotuses have to grow through murky waters in order to bloom. I had to grow and surrender to the murky waters in order to bloom and find myself.

Lotuses can survive climate extremes.

I have survived my own climate extremes of unstable moods, emotions, lifestyles, and harsh treatment from myself and from others.

Lotuses can die in extreme floods, but when waters recede, they always come back, because their seeds can survive for thousands of years.

Parts of me have died in the extreme floods of traumatic experiences, suicide attempts, and failed intentional heroin overdose attempts. But when waters receded, I came back. I kept going, because that's what we do.

I am a lotus in bloom.

You are also a lotus in bloom.

Lotuses are also living fossils that survived the Ice Age, the only plant in the northern hemisphere to do so.

For these reasons the lotus flower is special and is regarded as a symbol of enlightenment, self-regeneration, and rebirth. It's the perfect analogy for the human condition: even when its roots are grounded in the dirtiest, muddiest of waters, the lotus will rise to produce the most beautiful flower, no matter what.

It is a survivor.

I am a survivor.

You are a survivor.

So, the next time someone says anything to you about the way you are or how you look, let them.

You know your truth.

You know what it has taken for you to

survive. You know your mud. Be proud to have it beneath you for support, all mashed between your toes. Your mud makes you beautifully different, gives you strength, encourages growth, and provides the perfect foundation—the only foundation—for a blooming lotus to flourish. As women, we all have flourishing to do, in our own time.

Remember, if there is no mud, there is no lotus.

I am more than a Score

Macy Rushing

I struggled.

It took me awhile to admit it, because I was embarrassed. Even if I could go back and tell my fourteen-year-old self that it was going to be okay, I know I wouldn't have believed it. No one prepares you for growing up with a learning disability. Honestly, it's intimidating and overwhelming for a child to be labeled by doctors with all these scary terms and be written a bunch of prescriptions that are supposed to fix it.

I hated feeling different. I wanted a normal school year and summer. I dreaded school, loved it for social reasons, but hated how the medicine made me feel. At the school I attended, not only did you have to pass the classroom work and test, but also a state test.

The dreaded state testing.

Basically, they wanted to have perfect scores to show off they had the best school system in the state, so that everyone would move and enroll their kids there, blah, blah, blah. I'd pass the class, barely, but I'd pass. State tests were different. Failed or "unsatisfactory" or whatever nicer term they tried to label it that year, all still meant, "not good enough." That's not an easy word to read, *failed.* It's a heavy word that I let win over and over again.

Summer school: here I come.

I sacrificed my summer with friends in exchange for walking the halls freshman year with friends. While all my friends were having sleepovers and pool days, I couldn't do anything. I was dreading the final week of summer school; it meant it was time to retake that test.

Imagine the pressure we were feeling. I say we, because I wasn't alone. We all knew we weren't the smartest, but was it fair to categorize us all off of test scores? We were the low test scores. The underachievers.

Test week finally came around. Sweat beaded on my forehead as I sat for six hours a day, filling in bubbles on a Scantron and overthinking every answer.

How can one think positive about themselves when they've been looked at, and treated, so less-than? Some say they were helping, I don't doubt they thought they were. I simply wish people could remember their "less-than" moments during their "help." Because I know we've *all* experienced situations and struggles that caused us to feel not good enough.

The test was finally over, and of course to add to the stress, it would take weeks for the scores to come in. My friends were thrilled it was over, because then I could join the fun. However, mentally I couldn't relax unless I knew I would be with them in high school. While waiting for the results, I found out I made the junior varsity cheerleading squad. We went to cheer camp together, and I made more friends to enter into high school with. Everything started feeling like it was falling into place, but all the while I was still waiting on those scores.

One day, close to the date we were expecting the test results, a friend invited me over to spend the night. We had a great night and the next day her mother was very busy with work, which was fine. After getting a phone call, she popped up and said, "let's go get pizza." My friend and I were equally confused, but went with it. When we arrived back at her house, my mother was in the driveway. I had simply assumed I was going home, but as I got closer, I could see the worry on her face. I immediately knew what it meant without her saying one word. My knees got weak, and I slowly went to the ground. I really wasn't prepared to hear that word again. I went and packed up my stuff. I remember while I was packing, my friend's mom came to me with a shoebox. Inside were brand new wedges, very cute, but I wasn't really in the mood for a gift. Then she explained. As she was tearing up she said, "I want you to wear these. They make you feel tall, proud, and loved. Because no matter what that test says, you are above it all." I will never forget that moment.

It's hard to hear you failed again. You *know* you aren't a failure, but how else are you supposed to feel? I was going to be in my little brother's grade? I wasn't going to be a freshman with my friends? I wasn't going to be on the JV cheerleading squad?

Come to find out, I wasn't the only one that failed; there were many of us. So many that the school system worked together to figure out what could work for all of us. While it was still humiliating, the answer wasn't as bad as repeating the eighth grade. We were officially categorized as an "8.5." We were told we would get dropped off at the middle school in the morning, have a two-hour class, then a bus would bring me and other classmates to the high school for third through seventh hour. Once all the details were sorted out, I found out that since I wasn't fully a ninth grader I couldn't cheer on the JV squad after all. Before school even started, girls were asking me why I haven't been at practice. I didn't want to explain, because I had been overwhelmingly nervous about when the first person would ask.

What would I say? How would I explain something so serious without making myself sound stupid? I tried my best, but the reaction I always got in answer was a pitiful, "Oh."

I survived the first week. Overall, I was doing okay mentally, tried to focus on school, and not my student ID that had "8.5" in the grade slot. Second week of school was going well. Had a good routine, and my schedule wasn't bad. I was in my third hour class, and we had to walk to the computer lab for class that day. As I was walking with a childhood friend, all of a sudden the teacher walked by, tapped my friend on the shoulder and asked, "Hey, what did I tell you about talking to eighth graders?"

I held back the tears as I dropped my head in shame. It was the first time someone had made a comment about it. I knew the day would come, I just thought it would be from another student, not a teacher. I was more than shocked. More than humiliated.

The rest of the school year flew by. I eventually passed everything I needed to, and was on to the next grade. I was confused if I would labeled as being in grade "9.5," since I was a few credits behind, but they classified me as an official tenth grader, which meant I could participate in sports. I made the softball team and loved every minute. Sophomore year flew by, and junior year seemed much more intense. I was faced with more questions about the future. It was overwhelming because it seemed so far away for so long. Towards the end of junior year we all had to take the graduating exit exam, more to see where we all stood in overall scores. Obviously I was nervous because of my history with standardized tests, but I took it and felt great about it. All I could focus on was being a senior and having a locker in the senior hall. *Cool right?* Well, at least I thought so then. Now, I'm not sure why I cared.

It finally arrived, senior year! For the first day of school, I had a sleepover with my two best friends. We woke up together, and got all fixed up for the big day. Everything I went through up to that point seemed so worth it. On the sixth day into my senior year, I was pulled from class by an aid that read my test scores to me. It wasn't far out of the norm, so I wasn't worried, until she asked a teacher to leave her office to speak with me about it. The conversation started with the teacher explaining that I would need to be at school one hour early each day and stay one hour late, for tutoring.

I was confused. I thought, *How could I be failing anything six days into senior year?* I did not pass the exit exam, and I would get only one more chance to take it before graduation. If I didn't pass it then, I was told I would not be able to graduate. All the emotions from the eighth grade flooded into me again. As I walked out of her office I felt ... devastated. Was I ever going to overcome my learning disabilities? I went to the office and called my mom to check me out. She could hear in my voice something was wrong. Once I got to my car and found my cell phone, I called my mom again. The first thing I asked was, "Are we poor?" I knew more than anything I needed to get out of that environment. I just wanted to run, but I also felt the only way I would graduate on time was to transfer to a smaller, more attentive school, and private schools were the only option then.

Of course, I had to take a test to get in. I said my prayers and did the best I could, because honestly that's all I could do. I remember sitting with the principal of the new school in her office, nervous. She slowly looked up from my test, took her glasses off and politely said, "You scored below average." Of course I took a deep breath, looked around the room while rubbing the sweaty palms off on my pants. Then she said, "I want to ask you a question, what does respect and education mean to you?" I do not do well with being put on the spot, but I just spoke from my heart. As I started saying what they meant she seemed surprised, repositioned in her chair, and just smiled at me. I assumed she liked my answer. I smiled back, and in that moment, this stranger became my new principal, and I felt safe. It was okay, for the first time, that I scored below the average.

Senior year in that school was great. Since it was a smaller school, the classes were obviously smaller and as I had hoped, more attentive to helping me learn. I wasn't treated differently, or judged for asking more than one question in class if I was confused.

After I graduated, on time, I went to small community college. After the first year, I wanted out, and didn't think it was for me at all. It's very overwhelming, so I decided to take a year off from college. I worked two jobs and met my now husband. He motivated me to go back, so I did. I knew I could do it, and I did! It took me four years to get an associate's degree, but I DID IT! It was huge personal win for me!

Looking back, it's been a journey, one I'll never forget. It made me who I am now and I'm thankful for that. I don't look at struggles now, as overcoming something, but learning something. I believe it's so that we can relate, not necessarily overcome. Overcome means you've won, and I don't think any of us ever fully win over the feelings of being unworthy, because we experience those moments at different points in our life.

As a mother, I teach my kids that it's okay to ask questions if you do not understand. It's okay to not understand. If you see someone else struggling, help them.

Looking back, I wasn't a bully in middle school, but I definitely wasn't the nicest person. I can say that school year, my eighth-and-a-half year, humbled me. My attitude, before that year, was due to my feelings of being less-than, only it was something I could hide for the most part. In my eighth-and-a-half year, my deficiencies were public. The struggles I went through and the humiliation were all public, but now I'm very grateful for that.

Uplifting others is my anthem now. God provided people in my life to help lift me up in my darkest times. To believe in me. To stand by me. And ultimately to understand what it was like to feel unworthy.

Wearing the heels my best friend's mother gave me helped me hold my head high! My graduation principal took a chance on me for the person she saw inside of me, not a number. My parents supported me and never gave up on me. They were there through it all. My husband encouraged me to return to college, because he believed in me.

From struggling with learning disabilities to becoming a college graduate, a wife, and a mother, I don't feel smarter. I feel more empowered. This year, my first children's book will be published, and I was signed on a three-book deal. With all of it, I give God the praise.

I've learned I am not a score. I am more.

Don't be Told

Mikelyn Amphion

As many of us, I learned early in life of the male ego and the damage it can cause. Pulling our ponytails or punching us in the arm is just a few examples of the young, untethered male at work. I was sent out to navigate the world, without being equipped with the proper tools to protect my heart from that same ego. And let's face it, the physical domination that is so prevalent in their youth, mostly becomes psychological control in many male futures, if they aren't taught better.

We girls are told what behavior is acceptable and what is taboo. In class, I remember boys always acting silly and goofing off, and the teachers would say that they are just being boys. Yet, when a girl did the same thing, she was instantly frowned upon and often told how unladylike she was being. At that point in life, we are already learning our "place" in this world. Actions and comments like that are incredibly damaging to all genders.

Time goes by, and we start to enter adolescence ... relationships. This is when the already-set boundaries of being female start to really show. For most, we find ourselves stuck between a rock (being societal norms) and a hard place (being our own self-satisfaction). Oftentimes, I found myself leaning towards the rock, because that was what made most people happy.

We are taught to put aside our pride in order to be the "bigger person" and in order to "allow relationships to flourish." Still, nothing to do with our own happiness. I found that when I completely pushed aside the idea of having true fulfillment for myself, as dictated by the world, I attracted toxic people.

Just like all new things, those relationships looked shiny and perfect, because I was taught to overlook certain misgivings.

Unfortunately, many men are taught that their behaviour is normal, or better yet, justified. In the beginning, most women see the knight in shining armor, because we were programmed to overlook the bad. Many men typically focus on the negative in women, and are even programmed to notice any behavior that denotes "unladylike" traits.

In any relationship that progresses, we tend to share secrets in what we believe is a trusting relationship. In hopes that they accept you, right? In toxic relationships, as time goes on, their selfishness and control shows through more and more; not knowing that the secret you told them was the loaded weapon they so desperately needed. You find yourself confused about the interrogation you are under for being two minutes late getting home.

Most women have been in a relationship where they almost felt as though they needed to carry a stop watch to count down to the second so that they aren't "giving someone a reason to doubt." Logically, knowing that sometimes you hit traffic or walk at different speeds, this becomes a tragic cycle of fear.

Still, instead of walking away and accepting the red flags, I told myself a string of excuses to alleviate my own doubt. Sometimes, it seemed the only doubt my toxic person experienced was in believing the betrayal he'd made up in his own mind.

Nevertheless, women *learn* to protect the male ego, so that is exactly what we do. There would be days where things seem to be going right, but they'd fall apart in the blink of an eye. The moment I was happy, was the moment he would try to pick me apart. Every day I was reminded of the smallest mistakes I'd made. He always presumed everything I did was a blatant sign of disrespect towards him.

You're the extra character in the play of his life.

As they are telling you how wrong you are and how repulsive you are, they will counter it by asking something along the lines of "Aren't you glad I love you?" Because the woman ...Is just the side character.

It doesn't matter how you feel, because at the end of the day, it's the job of a woman to be the bigger person and to sweep things under the rug. We make excuses, constantly, for the behavior of our toxic partner. Becoming a broken record, always having some sort of reasoning as to why he said what he said, or did what he did. He was either drunk or had a bad day at work. We are taught it is likely our fault they behave the way they do. Then you feel the need to clean up for the both of you. Losing yourself day in and day out. Lying there in bed, wondering what peace is like.

It is never really about what you want to do, as long as his ego is taken care of, which means pleasing him in all ways possible. Women should never have to bow down to a man because society told her she is only worth what he values in her. By pleasing a man, and making her spouse happy, many also, unfortunately, still use that to value themselves. Just because something is written in the laws of society, does not make it right.

No matter how hard we try to be "good women," there is always that nagging voice in our heads telling us *this isn't right.* It is a constant teeter-totter between balancing the ways of society, wanting to be loved for who we are, and following God's word.

Little girls should not be *told* that only *he* can enjoy life. Women should not look in the mirror and cringe at the sight they see based off of what toxic, informal, societal rules tell her she is. Women should not have to be placed under interrogation, just because a guy has a self-inflicted guilty conscience or control issues.

Let's not forget the way we are viewed based on our emotions; you are either too emotional, or stone cold. You are either rude, because you didn't speak, or you are overly flirtatious because you did. Dead fish, or harlot. However, regardless of whatever you do, it can still be wrong, to the wrong person.

I pray that my future children will grow up with a sense of respect. I intend to instill it in them as best I can, with God leading me. My son will be taught the beauty and strength of women, as well as of men. My daughter will be taught she can use her voice without robbing a man of his. I will teach them both to set boundaries for those who have toxic tendencies, man or woman.

We, women, are such powerful beings, and it is not our job to be a door mat. God did not create us to be walked all over; He created us to be a part of something grand. To be who He created us to be in the world and be leaders in whatever it is we do. We are born with such exquisite qualities, and it is time to stop forcing ourselves to fit into a box created by others.

Our time to shine and thrive is now. You are amazing. Re-learn to not let toxic people, man or woman, tell you who you are. Don't let them try and rob you of yourself, or your joy.

Instead, let God lead and guide you. Be strong in who He created you to be, and never lose sight of your individual value and purpose.

I'm learning that very same thing, every day.

Let Her Talk

Mariah Jester-Wise

I wonder, with having the knowledge of all of the intricacies of being a woman, why do many women not have more understanding and gentleness with each other? Instead, we are competing over whose pregnancy was worse, who suffered harder from postpartum depression, whose period is harder, and so much more. It is disappointing, asking for help from a fellow woman, or just needing to vent, only for your problem to be dismissed by them. Sometimes, a venting session between two women is healing and can actually be a very funny way to bond with each other. However, there is a fine line between competing and comforting. Women need to understand that line, and remember that all a woman may need is for them to do one thing: let her talk.

A little bit about me, I have the Paragard copper IUD. Most women who have one probably cringe even just reading the name. For me, it has caused a plethora of problems since the day I got it inserted. Due to copper poisoning, I lost half of my hair within a couple of weeks. It has been five years, and it still has not fully come back. On top of that, it has caused me to have chronic migraines, severe abdominal cramps, my eyes have yellowed, and my periods are excruciatingly long and heavy. I go through at least a whole box of super plus and ultra tampons per cycle. My longest period to date was twenty two days...

Now, I'm not the only one. I've learned that those side effects are not uncommon for that device. The effects can be so cripplingly painful that oftentimes I can't sleep, and if I do manage to get to sleep, I get awakened and have to soak in an almost boiling tub of water, just to ease the pain. It has also caused other issues like worsened anxiety and panic attacks, depression, mood swings, full body fatigue, painful sex, severe heart palpitations that make me drop to my knees, even my memory has gotten worse. I can't focus on anything anymore. So, I decided to go to the doctor.

My mother-in-law has told me, whenever you plan on going to the doctor for female issues, request a male doctor. I wasn't fully comfortable with the thought of a male doctor talking to me about issues they couldn't possibly understand, and I definitely was not comfortable with the thought of a male looking at me in such a vulnerable position, so I stupidly requested a female to help me. She was indeed very helpful, until I mentioned that my problems are because of my period. Suddenly, she was being short, callous, dismissive, and just plain rude. She stopped asking questions, started to condescend me, and belittled my pain. I tried to continue talking about it, because I desperately needed help. However, she told me that she thought I was exaggerating and that I needed to suck it up, because "we women all have the same issues." Then she went on about how bad her periods are and her friends' periods and just about every other woman she's close to. Not once did I try and make it seem like my periods are worse than every other woman's

109

in the world; I know every woman has their own worst days. All I was trying to do was get some kind of aid for mine. Honestly, I got a little irritated that my doctor's appointment got hijacked by other women who weren't even in the room. I directly asked if I could just get some kind of prescription-strength medicine, even if it were only something similar to, but stronger than Midol, and she bluntly said, "No. Every woman has a period. You can use over-the-counters just like everyone else."

Feeling as though I had no choice, especially since doctor's visits weren't refundable, I shyly said "Okay," and walked out feeling embarrassed and angry.

Thinking about it from a different perspective, you will most likely never hear of a story about a male going to a male doctor for a male-specific problem and being told he can't be helped because others suffer with it too. That their stories directly affect how his issue will be assessed and treated.

There should be no better match than a female medical professional and a female patient who needs help. But for some reason, it took me going to a male doctor, who would have no capacity of physically understanding my pain, to get the help I was asking for. He told me that I had copper poisoning and that it could be very dangerous if left untreated.

He helped me.

The female doctor seemed subconsciously competitive with me and didn't bother to look further into my problem. Unfortunately, this is such a common problem, but it runs deeper than the medical field.

We women have this behavior at the social level.

At work a few years later, on a particularly rough day of my cycle, I was helping a coworker when she said that I didn't look well and asked what was wrong. At work I talked very little about my personal life, especially since I was their supervisor, and I had to keep it professional, but she seemed genuinely concerned. I was so exhausted with my painful periods and felt maybe just telling her about it would help. I started to decompress and vent; not even a full sentence into me letting it out, she interrupted and started telling me how bad her period gets. I was annoyed, but I listened and gave whatever advice that I could. Because, hey, we do all need an outlet. We all need to talk. Then, another female coworker came up to us and asked what we were talking about.

"Oh, I was just saying how bad my period

is," the first girl said, to which the second coworker excitedly and eagerly chimed in. She went on about how hers "feels like she's being stabbed by a fiery knife with thorns on it."

What had begun as unprompted concern for my wellbeing had devolved into what seemed like a competition between my two coworkers. After a minute or two of hearing the back-and-forth, I walked away and got back to work. They didn't even notice I'd left the conversation. Now, I did not ask for attention, but once it was given to me, I opened up to fellow females about something bothering me. As soon as it was revealed that it was in relation to menstruation, concern and care became callousness and belittling.

And instead of an outlet, I was left feeling like my issues were even less important. It was extremely disheartening, because simply saying that you're having a hard time with your period, just being able to let it out to another female and seeing that she understands, can sometimes be all the help you need to get through the day.

This all seems so negative, but this leads me to my final story. My husband and I were at the store, about to check out, when an older woman in front of us saw that all we had on the belt was my period essentials: Midol, Tylenol, Pamprin, the largest pack of super-plus tampons, and special dark chocolate (and maybe a few more yummy snacks). She looked at me, saw my pale, anemic skin, puffy eyes, and fatigued hunched body and asked, "My goodness, are you alright?"

"Yes, I'm fine, haha. Thank you, though," I said.

"No really, you seem like you aren't doing alright. How bad is it?" she insisted.

"It's just my period, it's a little bad today, gotta buy the goodies!" I laughed, attempting to disregard it, as so many others had.

The old woman pursed her lips and laughed, looking at me with a mixed look of amusement and familiar frustration, "Sweetheart, your period should not be so bad that you look so sick. You should really get checked out, because something is wrong. I hope you feel better!"

I'll definitely be keeping that woman in my memories. It makes me smile every time I think about it; she had such concern for a woman she didn't know, and she only wanted me to feel better. She didn't try to compete, didn't compare, and didn't disregard. I didn't ask for it, and it was certainly no cure, but it helped. The sentiment made me feel better, and the rest of the day felt just a little easier with her support.

If we women could all take Psalm 46:5[9] and keep it in our minds when speaking with each other, being there for each other, not letting females feel like their problems are a burden or inconvenience, I think it would be a much better world to live in as a female.

It's a tough world for all of us; we need to support each other, not try and out-do each other. Females should all come together and help each other with the thing we all have in common: being a woman.

Let us remember that if another woman comes to you, feeling unwell, going through her worst pain, and wanting to vent, let her talk.

9. Psalm 46:5.

Puzzles and Constants

Tia Wade

My mother always told me when I was growing up to follow my first instinct. I've been told we were born with intuition. Seemingly something small, yet so loud in your heart, intuition can lead you away from harm, whether physical or emotional. Still, it's up to you to choose to listen to yourself.

In my senior year of college, I was put to the test. I met a man that went against the grain, and my intuition told me to stay away. I didn't listen. He raped me and left me alone on the streets for my best friends to find me. Walking around waiting for rescue in an unfamiliar place, the only thing I could think of was my mother's voice, "You knew better! From start to finish you saw the signs and still did what you wanted!"

I did know better, I just didn't do better.

The signs were all there. From the way that he unnervingly played the same song for the entire ride to the way that he sped around the lakes of New Orleans as if it was his last night as a free man.

If only I paid a little more attention.

These thoughts repeated in my head, over and over, until I saw that familiar blue car drive up with my two best friends inside. Everything was a daze until I made it to the hospital. I never remembered telling my friends what happened, but I didn't have to.

Words could not explain how my family felt, finding me in that hospital at 2 a.m. when I was just recently in my dorm "preparing for bed." My mother's eyes were red, my sisters' hands were shaking, and my friends stared at the floor pensively. I was numb and a mess at the same time. When Mom walked into the room, she showed the strength of a thousand armies. She shut it all down, "Stop it! Breathe! Take a minute and get it together. Things need to get done so we can go home."

Harsh? Most definitely. Yet it was exactly what I needed. The tears, the panic attacks, all of it was over, and I was calm enough to finish this excruciating process.

After that, I became withdrawn from life. I couldn't get out of my head. I felt as though I had no light. I had decided that I couldn't trust myself to make proper decisions in keeping myself safe. With that thought process I went back home to Baton Rouge to be in a safe space. A place where I didn't have to worry about my surroundings or people's intentions. I gave up on leaving my room unless it was a therapy session or one of the five baths I had started taking each day.

I was content with where I was, sheltering myself from the world, but of course I had to come in contact with the others at some point, right? Not long after, my mother's childhood friend was getting married, and I was told we had to participate in the wedding. Not only was my little sister the flower girl, but I still wasn't comfortable being home alone, so the choice was essentially made for me. The day of the wedding, I sat, dressed, hiding in the den behind the bar. I couldn't get out of my head

117

enough to be around people. I felt like a child hiding from their parents so they didn't have to go to Sunday school or something. Mother found me, brushed my hair up, straightened the outfit she had bought me for the occasion, and we were off.

We made it to the venue, and I stayed secure next to my little sister, fifteen years younger and the only strength I had at that moment. She always had and always will have my heart. I remember thinking I would do or be anything I could for her, which apparently included pretending to have my life together, when it felt so far from the truth. I stayed with her until I heard the bride's song start, then I found my seat next to my mother.

Everything was so beautiful, yet I couldn't get out of my head.

Ever since I was three, the bride and her children have been in my life, so I felt safe there. I also felt like the only broken person in the room; the deflated life raft in a sea full of happily floating party barges. They were all so happy—dancing and drinking until their hearts were content.

And I just couldn't get out of my head.

That was until my constant, the bride's son, came over to me. Knowing Kristopher since we were three made him a constant in my life. We went to school and graduated together. We hadn't talked often over the years, but we hadn't needed to. He was a constant.

"That's What I Like" by Bruno Mars was playing, and Kristopher asked me to dance. He made a funny face, and I used my ugliest laugh as I grabbed his hand. I let him lead me to the dance floor for what I thought would be one song. We danced for hours! Being with him was, and still is, like being in our own little goofy and upbeat world. The only time we stopped was when it was time to throw the bouquet. The DJ asked for all the single ladies. Kristopher placed his foot in front of me, "Not for long," he said. We simply stared at each other until the music came on again initiating another round of dancing.

In those moments, standing there with Kristopher, I was out of my head.

Suffice to say after drinking and dancing for so long, I wasn't exactly in the right state of mind, so when it came time to put my new number in his cracked iPhone that I could barely see through, I put in the wrong numbers.

Even though when he realized it and had felt I may have played him, he didn't give up.

Kristopher took a liking to all of my posts.

It wasn't until I made a post about one of my favorite musicals, that I realized that he was trying to get my attention. Leaping on faith I sent him a message. After clearing up the misunderstanding, he asked me out on a date.

My whole world stopped.

The rape replayed in my head, and all I could think was, *Can I trust him? Can I trust myself?* Somehow, I believed he understood my hesitation. After turning down so many people and their invitations, something about this one felt different. He never pushed too hard, and that meant a lot to me.

I decided to do something different.

I followed my heart and intuition. I said yes.

To this day I am proud of myself for trusting myself and allowing someone, anyone, in after the rape. He suggested we go somewhere public, so we decided on dinner and the remake of *Beauty and the Beast.* He said he would pick me up from my best friend's house, and we would take it from there.

While on the date, I checked in by text with my best friend constantly at the beginning of the night. It wasn't until Kristopher and I were headed to the theater after dinner, that I realized that those messages had grown further and further apart. The entire ride to the theater, he played music he thought I wouldn't know. But to his surprise, we ended up singing them together, word-for-word.

Once the movie was over, we still didn't want the night to end ... so he bought a puzzle. Puzzles had always been something we both did growing up. We went back to his home where he lived with his older brother, played some music, and started the puzzle.

That spoke volumes to me.

He didn't expect too much from me, he never pushed me, and he let me make my own decisions that I felt safe with. He only wanted me to be comfortable.

Four years later, he is still my constant. In all of those years, no matter what his role was in my life, I realize he'd always had my back. He was always the one to put a smile on my face no matter the situation. Bad grades, bad boyfriends, or even the death of my grandmother, he was always there. I feel safe with him and am no longer in my head over the past.

...Eight puzzles later, and we will be getting married later this year.

I Remember

Anonymous

I pleaded, "I'm a virgin."
Words I would repeat in my mind over and over throughout my young life. I said a few other words, but "no" wasn't one of them. I cried, tried pushing him off of me, and I scratched at his face. I begged, "Please," but still ... I don't remember ever actually saying the word "no."

A word that would haunt me for years.

The next morning, I woke with a black eye, a bruised ribcage, which now I know was likely a fractured or cracked rib or two, and bruises over most of my body. My neck had finger marks and my breasts had scratches on them where he'd torn my shirt away.

For weeks, because of the ribs, I would walk slowly and be in constant pain. When Mom asked me the next morning what happened, I just said, "softball." Her accepting that answer so readily was both relieving and disappointing. Even with all the pain I was in, it didn't compare to the mental anguish I went through. I thought of every detail I could muster. Every word he said with a laugh. Every word I said through tears.

Still, in all of that, *I don't remember saying the word "no."*

I remember freezing in fear.

I remember it was cold outside, but I was sweating.

I remember being in shock that it was really happening.

I remember hearing him laugh throughout the attack.

I remember getting into the shower and being surprised that the only blood on my body was a trail of dried spots where he'd scratched me. I thought I'd find blood between my legs, but there wasn't any. I'd always heard that the first time there was always blood, but turns out that isn't true.

I remember thinking I would never jog alone again at night for the rest of my life, even though I had done it for years around our neighborhood.

I also remember I couldn't tell anyone but my brother. He and I are close, he'd practically raised me anyway, since my parents were usually both drunk at night, and I can honestly say if it weren't for that relationship I may have hated all men.

"No" is a word I quickly learned to use afterward. I was harsh with others, whereas before that day, I had been a pushover. I heard, "You used to be so sweet," or "You aren't acting like yourself," so many times that I started laughing internally when people would say them to me. With time, those words lost their power. I also lost a lot of friends, especially the boys. Maybe I really *was* "sweet," before, as so many of my guy friends would say, but I didn't feel sweet anymore.

I learned quickly that if you don't play nice, people scatter.

I often wondered, when so many people noticed such a huge change in me, why didn't any of them try to help? Why did they only get upset because I wasn't being who they needed me to be? Why was being uncomfortable around me, more important than me?

My brother tried to help by asking me to go with him out to meet friends, or even just him and me to a movie, but again my answer was always "no."

With the two friends left who did still call every now and then, the answer was "no." Eventually, they stopped calling. "No" was not only my answer to everything, but it was also my heart's answer.

Did I want to go with Mom to get my hair done? *No.*

Did I want to go to the grocery store? *No.*

Did I want dinner? *No.*

New clothes? *No.*

Live? ...*No.*

Then, one day, my brother came back from going out with friends and asked if he could share something with me. He was my best friend, my only real friend left, so of course I said yes.

He'd been to a revival that night and he'd given his life to God. My parents were against anything like that in our house, probably because they drank so much and didn't think God would love them. I kind of understood it, because I was so angry, I thought maybe God wouldn't love me either. My brother shared with me. He didn't give up on me, and he would always share God with me in a loving way that made me crave to know God and "be free." He had certainly changed in great ways. He talked about joy and peace. He'd gotten a scholarship to a college in Arkansas and didn't want to leave me, but I told him I was better and that he had to go. The moments spent with my brother were a reprieve sometimes from the emptiness, but when he left for college, the reprieve followed him. We'd talk on the phone, but it wasn't the same. I'd faked being better for him, so he wouldn't feel like he abandoned me.

Sitting in my closet one night, crying and alone, I was thinking over *that night* and feeling all of those same emotions that constantly weighed on me. Guilt about not actually saying the word "no" was at the top. For some reason I felt I deserved what happened to me, because I hadn't said actually said the word "no."

That word had cost me so much. I'd lost friends, what little relationship I did have with my parents, my grades suffered, my health suffered from all the weight loss, and I had little self-worth. I had lost ME, not the old me, because when I thought on it, the old me was the one who didn't say "no," but the new me said "no" all the time, and it still didn't help. I still didn't have anything that made me feel like ME.

That night, in the closet, with nothing left but thoughts of dying, I cried out to God for help.

I remember saying "God, I don't even know if you know me, but you know my bother, and he loves you. He thinks you will love me too, and I think I need it." I remember pausing, crying, waiting for something to happen, hoping ... but there was nothing. Then I remembered what my brother said about Jesus, so I asked God to forgive me of everything I'd ever done, and wash me in the blood of Jesus. The floodgates, I didn't know were closed, opened and I poured out all my hurt and pain to God.[10] All of my guilt. All of my anger. The confusion. The unworthiness. For hours I cried out all of my parents' drinking and abandonment. All of their fights. I cried for my brother being gone.

I had cried so much in my life, but it never really gave me the relief it was supposed to give me, it had only added more sad memories to my life. But that night, crying my heartache out to God, I felt lighter. I asked God to help me find a life again.

I started to feel relief.

I understood peace for the first time in my life. That one night didn't take everything away; however, it gave me hope of something more than the pain.

Truth is, nearly ten years later, I still cry out to God for healing. I am slowly finding the ME that I want to be, and I realize that will keep changing. When those feelings hit me, which happen further and further apart as time goes on, I cry through it and ask God for help again. And I feel Him there, easing my suffering and giving me hope.[11]

He's building a *me* on the inside.

My brother helped me enroll in a community college near where he and his wife live. I'm still in the I-don't-know-phase of where I am going, but I trust God does, and I am following.

My dad died hating God, but my mother got saved not long after his death. We are finding a relationship we never had before, and I am finding forgiveness for her. I sometimes imagine her, after my father's passing, like I had been, sitting in my old closet, crying and alone, and wanting to die. I remember imagining her fear of what was going to happened to her now that she had to survive and work and be alone.

I've learned that she had trauma of her own from her childhood, not so far off from my own trauma, which she had never been able to deal with. With God's help, my mom quit drinking. She looks younger than she ever has, and I am happy getting to know the HER that is evolving.

I realize not everything requires a definitive "yes" or "no," but some things do. I still say "no," and that's healthy. I also say "yes," too—to life and happiness. To the same forgiveness and mercy that God showed me, even if I have to picture everyone in my old closet, crying and alone, and wanting to die.

I think I've found a healthy balance to my yeses and nos, but I'll always remember the best "yes" that I have ever said, and ever will, was in that closet when I said yes to God.

10. Psalm 34:17
11. Jeremiah 29:11

Metamorphosis

Alexis Ranea Jester

Everyone has a metamorphosis stage in their life. I feel like some people go through it smoothly! Others, not necessarily. For me, I think my big metamorphosis phase was going through, and overcoming my abuse.

I saw the red flags. Like, I know I did. I must have, right?

I had all the people closest to me warn me, and try to "help" me, but that only made me push them away. It was never consciously, but if you have ever been in an abusive relationship, you understand. It's crazy the way your point of view flips and you protect the abuser. I don't want to talk too much about the abuse part itself, that's not this story.

This is the story of a caterpillar.

I've had the beautiful blessing of having so many people share testimonies of their abuse with me, and for them I am eternally grateful. Once I heard from other people's mouths that they experienced what I did, or something similar, it made me feel supported, seen, and assured. It really did make me feel less alone and less foolish. I was fortunate enough to have so much support, people who listened when I needed, and I feel like it made me somewhat prepared for the emotional rollercoaster that comes with the recovery from abuse.

I was warned how much I would miss him, and the effects of Stockholm syndrome. I was warned that I would have troubles being alone, and warned I would have to essentially unlearn all the behaviors and fears he engrained into me for years. Having to focus all my energy on what he wanted, approved of, and would allow me to do. Being blind to how codependent I had been, how I was no longer me. I was, but I wasn't. I was unrecognizable, even to me. Melted down to just my cells.

I was prepared for having friends that didn't want to rekindle after the time I'd spent shut away in my chrysalis phase.

In regards to recovering, I feel what I was the least prepared for when I finally got out of my abusive relationship was the true loneliness that settles when you are left alone with yourself ... and you have no idea who that person is anymore. Then, realizing no one else knows who that person is anymore either.

If you are lucky, you will have those select few friends you refused to let go of, which is hard! Or friends that your abuser "approved" of. Some friends will never understand fully what you went through. Let's be honest, you had to keep them in the dark about most of it, or when you did tell them (and they told you to leave) you got defensive and protective of your abuser. No one really talks about how emotionally taxing it is to keep in contact with people when you are isolated and torn down constantly, if you are allowed to.

For me, these few friends that I kept in contact with kept me feeling like I was still in touch with me. Between them and my parents, they were the tree branches that anchored me. Even when I didn't realize it.

When you do choose to hold onto friends

and family, your abuser will do whatever they can to plant seeds of doubt and hate in your mind. If they can't make you cut them off, they'll trick you into doing it yourself.

Those friends that I held onto stuck around well into my recovery; some have stayed to this day. They were there for my mood swings, my meltdowns, and my lashing out. They let me spew out the disgusting accusations that had been buzzing around like a swarm of angry wasps in my head for months, or years, after the eggs he left in my mind finally hatched. A few times, I had to just let the thoughts out, and confront people. And of course, all this did was hurt them. At the time, I desperately needed to get these thoughts out! I had to start sifting through the rubble and finding out what parts were actually me ... and what parts were him.

In hindsight, my friends and family didn't deserve to clean up the mess he made.

Once I made it away, I thought, *So now I'm finally free.*

Right?

I could finally do things that brought me joy. Things I loved, things I wanted to do! Only, I didn't know how to do anything I was once good at and enjoyed before. Talents, skills, and hobbies need practice and reinforcement.

Nothing I missed was easy to me.

I reached out to friends to hang out and started slightly feeling like myself again! Then I realized, in the two years I'd been molded into someone unrecognizable, many of my friends had spent that same two years growing as people, making new friends, finding new interests I've never even heard of. They had already become butterflies and their advice was that one day I would be one, too ... once I became "me" again.

I still felt stuck in a cocoon.

Not only did I have to unlearn everything, not only did I have to recover from the ache and learn to not need him or miss him, not only did I have to rebuild my shattered life, but I found myself having to relearn my skills and hobbies, find myself again, and then reintroduce myself to my best friends. I looked at some of them in the face and I knew: this is my person! My sister! They have been here!

So, why are we complete strangers?

For few of these beautiful friends that still stand by me, I can say, my bond is stronger with them now than it ever has been in all the years I've known them. Sadly, a few of my best friends, ones that stuck through the abuse, the isolation and me pushing them away, the ones that stood strong through my hurricane of emotion, couldn't handle the unfamiliarity and discomfort of meeting the new me. But in a way, that shell around me was a means of survival. I needed that phase. To heal, to grow.

Once the smoke cleared and I was "sane" again, they were ready to run to, hug, and spend time with the old me, the "me" before him. Instead, they met a stranger, and it's okay. As painful as it was, I eventually understood that this stranger isn't what they signed up for.

And really, it is okay.

After you recover from abuse, you have a new standard for how people will treat you. You are made aware of abuse and manipulation tactics that you never noticed before, and you see it in people you love. Not as bad, of course! Typically, they don't do it intentionally. For me, I started to become vocal about my feelings and what I wouldn't tolerate for the first time. Me saying that something hurt my feelings, or saying I don't like being talked to a certain way, or called certain names, etcetera, was not comfortable for people who knew me as a "no offense taken," fun-loving, pushover. People tend to get very defensive when you vocalize that something they do or say hurts your feelings, triggers you, or bothers you. Even if you aren't mad at them, correcting them, or telling them they did anything intentionally wrong! I don't ask people to apologize for something they didn't do intentionally or didn't "mean it that way" (which is a big one), but I no longer have a problem speaking up and saying I don't like it or it hurt me. There is nothing wrong with this. People who love abused people have to change too, and some people aren't willing to. Now though, I only have space in my life for people who are open and honest emotionally, and are willing to hold themselves responsible for their actions—intentional or not. To me, this is healthy communication. Some people think I'm too sensitive now. I think I'm stronger now than ever, because I can stand up for myself. For that, I will never be sorry.

As much as it hurts, the people that want to go ... let them go. The people that want you to be that who you were before, your "old you," aren't willing to make those changes.

Everyone goes through metamorphosis, in their own way. Be proud of yourself if you are or as you watch your old friends shed their chrysalis! Be happy for them as they become their new selves and they take flight, even if it's far away from you.

As much as you'll miss them, it's okay to

come out of your chrysalis and find out ...
you've been a moth all along.

You don't need to chase after butterflies.

You will find other moths along your way.

Self-Conscious Does not Mean Silent

Megan Taunton

As a woman, I can look back on my youth and see how much self-consciousness and self-doubt robbed me of a voice. It robbed me of opportunities and experiences.

One thing that brought me confidence in my teenage years was being a part of a dance team. Dancing gave me so much joy and for someone who really struggled with worth, it was one thing I truly felt confident at. Young women have a lot of things thrown at them in this world, from how to look, how to act, what to say, what size we should be, how we should parent. There are so many things thrown at us, or labels placed upon us, that we get weighted down to the point where when we look in the mirror we have to wipe away those labels like wiping the fog from the mirror after a hot shower. We wipe and wipe until our arms get tired from the motion, and we simply give up.

What's the use?

There are moments in our life when we feel passionate about a topic or we feel the sting of emotion when we hear or read something. That first instinct we want to speak out or speak up, but then we quickly realize, *I'm just me. What do they care what I have to say,* or *Who am I kidding, I can't do that.*

That has been me so many times over the years. I would feel this burning inside and such pull to speak up, to share something, to give my perspective, but ended up shying away from it. Day-to-day conversations felt awkward for me; I remember times in my life when I would rehearse what I would say in certain situations to keep from looking like a total bumbling idiot. I usually ended up stuttering words and feeling so stupid that I wouldn't talk at all.

I think my deep roots into self-doubt

stemmed from not knowing who I was, not knowing my purpose, and definitely from living in fear. Sure I had talents and interests and goals, but nothing notable that helped me feel purposeful. I knew the norm was to graduate college, work, get married, start a family, and live happily ever after.

My life took a very quick turn when our oldest daughter was diagnosed with a terminal brain tumor; I found out very quickly that I had no room to give into self-doubt when it came to making decisions for her and for our family. My faith took root and was no longer floating on the surface waiting to be pulled and tossed.

The roots traveled down deep and anchored.

I began to see my inner doubts diminish and a walk of blind faith begin. I was given a platform through social media to share my daughter's journey and also our faith to thousands of people. When we were interviewed or asked questions, I became her voice. While I felt completely unequipped to speak and felt the *who am I* feeling, I also tapped into what God had been nudging me to do all along; and that was to allow the Holy Spirit to speak through me, to give Him my weakness and self-doubt and allow Him to use it.

The more time I put into feeling things,

analyzing things, and writing things down, God helped me sort out emotions and also sort out purpose. If I felt these things as a woman, a mom, a wife, then I know that others must feel them as well. Maybe my words on a computer screen could lift another up, someone may relate to us ... who am I to say no to God?

So I continued writing. I wrote about my grief, my children, and my struggles and triumphs as a follower of Jesus. I pushed the self-consciousness away and started finding who I was in Christ, who He made me to be. I put the time in with Him ... and I found Megan.

Writing on social media is one thing, I love writing devotional-type posts or sharing my struggles. I also enjoy sharing my daily life and laughing at myself, but recently I've found myself wanting to speak. Like speaking words into the world, and sometimes writing your thoughts and speaking them come out so different. In my car, some time ago when I was doing home health work, I got tired of static radio stations in the country so I would listen to a podcast on my phone. They were pretty new to me, but they seemed to be a growing in popularity. One day, I felt a nudge to start a podcast.

What?! Me? For real? Are you sure?

I had absolutely no clue how to do a podcast, but I felt a strong passion and pull towards it. So I did my research and just happened upon a "startup" class for beginners at a very reasonable price, and I jumped on it. The purpose of it just rolled out as if God knew it was meant to be all along. Topics were created, and I felt like so much of what I wanted or needed to say for a lifetime was about to be unleashed. I guess it is true what you say as you age: you really can look back and analyze your past, your past behaviors, and grow from it.

Experiencing the death of my daughter and grief brought out so many questions, yet also clarified so much about life and loss. I knew my podcast must be called, *Life & Loss with Megan Taunton.* Its goal was to openly talk about my life experiences and my losses—that despite our loss, we can still live a vibrant life. I wanted my love and passion to pierce the ears of my listeners and ultimately pierce their heart leading them to a closer walk with Christ.

Today the podcast has more downloads than I ever anticipated, and I have so much fun with it. I am far from professional with most of my podcast episodes. It's simply me sitting cross legged on my bed with my laptop and microphone propped up on pillows, but in those moments when I am speaking, I feel alive with Christ's words flowing from my mouth. Every fiber in me ignites as I let my mind run free. So many years wasted of me staying silent, when I should have said hello to that person in the grocery store, or when I should have shared my story, stood up for myself. I think of the example I want to set for my kids; self-doubt, and self-consciousness doesn't belong in our lives, but unfortunately they are there.

God made us in His image with the powers to sort through thoughts and an awareness to search for who we were made to be. Not everyone will create a social media page or a podcast, but we can use our "voices," even in action, in so many ways that are around us every day.

Search for it, listen for it, and He will use you in ways you never thought possible. You know what they say ... when a woman of Christ finds her voice, devil watch out!

Step by Step

Nicole Brice

May 2013 will forever stick out in my mind. That was when my life was turned upside down. I remember it like it was yesterday. I had not been feeling well for weeks, and I just knew something was not right. I remember begrudgingly buying a pregnancy test at the local Wal-Mart while I was out in Hazlehurst, Mississippi for work. I was thirty-two and at the top of my career. *I surely don't want to be pregnant*, I told myself.

I didn't take the test right away after buying

it. I knew I had to hold onto it for later in the evening when my husband wasn't going to be home, because I was scared. Was I, the woman who didn't want children, pregnant? Later that evening, everything would change. Even then I still had no clue just how much.

That evening, I sat down with *The Breakfast Club* on TV. I waited, went outside, and then finally wrestled with the thoughts flowing through my brain to find the courage to take "the" test. As I waited for the results, sitting on the bathroom floor with my Chihuahua, Abbie, looking up at me wagging her tail, nervously biting my nails, I saw the test start coming to life. First, one line appeared ... and then the other ... survey says, "Pregnant!"

I looked at the test in shock for what seemed like well over twenty minutes. I Googled all possible combinations of the test being false.

I sat.

I thought.

I contemplated my next steps.

I gave in and texted one of my best friends at the time to talk to her. I needed her expertise. She had just found out a few months prior that she, too, was pregnant. Everything she and I talked about pointed to me being definitely pregnant. She and I spoke of a plan to tell my husband. It was the perfect plan.

The next morning, with Abbie on my lap, the pregnancy test on the hubby's night stand, and me holding a sign that said, "I'm going to be a big sister." There I was, sitting on our bed, as he awoke on a Saturday morning.

"What's going on?" he said while still half asleep.

I simply held up the sign and then grabbed the test and held it up and said nothing. All he could muster out was a simple, "Seriously?" Then it turned into him saying, "No way, no way..." over and over again. I kept confirming to him that this was it. I was pregnant.

The following week, I met with my doctor who formally confirmed the pregnancy. Most women would be ecstatic knowing they are bringing a life into this crazy world. I was scared—scared beyond words.

Our son made his entry on January 9, 2014, which was two weeks early. I suffered from high blood pressure, and the doctor had to induce me early to ensure the safety of the baby. From the start, he was a tiny, little guy.

Five pounds and thirteen ounces of cuteness.

I was in love. I cried and vowed to be the best mom no matter what, even if I hadn't a clue what I was doing in regards to motherhood.

I was clueless about being a mom. I had grown up primarily around adults or older children. I have a brother, but of course, he's older than me, so being around young children just never was my thing. I didn't even babysit as a teenager, if that tells you anything.

Could I even do this?

From the start, our son was a difficult baby. From latching issues to issues with food textures, something just wasn't right, and I sensed it pretty early on.

When other children our son's age started reaching the basic milestones and our son wasn't, I wondered if there was something bigger than just "not right." At eighteen months old, the owner of the daycare keeping our son called me into her office to talk. She started telling me about the strange behaviors she's observed in our son and how she believed he had a severe speech delay in comparison with the other children attending the daycare. I always knew his speech wasn't where it needed to be for his age, but his pediatric doctor kept assuring me that it was only a delay and that milestones are simply a guideline. He reassured me that our son was fine and would "get there." Months went by, and our son wasn't getting there.

147

Therapies for our son started right around the time he was twenty months old. He started receiving Speech and Occupational Therapy once a week. They would come to his daycare and pull him out of class to administer the therapy. I was highly optimistic. I still did not accept that anything major was wrong ... even though, in my gut, I knew it was.

Fast track to May 2017, and we've had our son in countless therapies for the past few years, with no improvement. No speech. No "mama," no "dada,"... nothing. Not to mention, the unwavering energy from this child who runs laps no matter where we go. By the time I got pregnant with our daughter, we'd been to every doctor in the state imaginable—even a child Psychologist—and still no one could provide us answers on what is wrong with our son.

After a thirty-minute visit with a Neurologist, she proceeds to tell us he's Autistic with severe Childhood Apraxia of Speech. The only guidance she offered was writing us a prescription for ABA therapy, which she said would help him to speak.

The Child Development doctor was the next one to sign off on my son's Autism diagnosis with no formal test, nothing. He was just going with what the Neurologist had already said.

In July of 2017, my son started his ABA therapy. It was only a few days after I had given birth to my daughter. In addition to this, I was working full-time, so my husband was the one shuffling him back-and-forth each day until I was able to get out and about. It was a grueling program 9 a.m.-3 p.m. each day of nothing but ABA therapy in a school-like setting. In addition to his ABA therapy, he was also still attending Speech and OT in the mornings before ABA. It was non-stop therapy for our little boy.

We started to see minimal progress upon beginning the extensive ABA therapy program, but nothing significant that we could celebrate. I began to sink into a deep depression. Not only were my hormones completely out of whack from having just given birth, but here I was with a newborn and a toddler-aged autistic child who wasn't making progress.

For the rest of the year, I continued shuffling my son to his therapies, taking care of my newborn daughter, and working. I cried daily. I cried while driving. I cried while in the shower. I could not stop crying no matter how hard I tried. Eventually, I joined a support group on social media made up of mothers with children in the same boat as mine. It was refreshing to be able to vent to these ladies about my struggles with my son and they understood! They got it!

They knew exactly what I was experiencing and had I not had that support group during that time, I would have probably become even more depressed. However, instead I became hopeful. Those ladies lifted me up and assured me that we were all in this together and all looking for answers for our children. We were also all doing all we could to help them progress. Also, that my feelings, the negative ones that plagued my conscious, were okay.

With the chaos surrounding my son and new daughter, I thought I would be forced to quit my career completely, because there was no way I could continue to work full-time and pull all of this off, too. The owner of my company agreed to let me work from home rather than the company lose me altogether. He set no definitive time frame as to how long I could do this, and everything was still positive on the job front. He said he didn't want me to have any added stress. Unfortunately, that wasn't true. My job wasn't secure enough, and to my complete and utter mortification, I was soon replaced.

Now, our son has been in ABA therapy since 2017 and in Speech and OT since far before that. He is seven years old with the mentality of a three-year-old. Limited speech still. And, yet, we still hold out the hope of many parents with Autistic children: hope he will speak and hope he will be able to live a full, happy life.

I see other children progressing at his age, so I refuse to give up. I will waiver, because I am human. However, I've learned to cope with my depression. I want to focus on being the best mom I can be to my two beautiful children. I am not ashamed to say that I had to seek outside help for myself. In order to function fully as a mom, I need to be well mentally, and I took the time to seek out the necessary resources to ensure I could function each day without a meltdown. I may no longer have a career with that company, but I have something better. I started my own consulting firm where I work with musicians, brands, and a host of incredible people. I've got a wonderful husband and two loving children by my side.

Our son has such a sweet nature, and I enjoy each and every one of his hugs ... even when he accidentally chokes me. I've learned in my thirties, so far, to *never* give up. God has a plan for everything and everyone.

From struggles with my son to struggles with my own professional identity, I've learned to maintain a positive outlook for the most part.

I pray daily, and God gives me strength.

Some days I'll break.

But then, I'll compose myself again, and I'll move onward.

Walking Through

Michelle James

Most people call me Mimi. When I was four years old, my mom died. That in itself is traumatic for a young child; however that's when my struggles really began.

I had no one else to take me, so I was placed in the foster care system. I was in and out of foster care for four long years.

When I was eight, I was fortunate enough to be adopted. I remember knowing that being adopted was the prize, the ultimate. Also, that being adopted meant I was wanted and valued.

However, I wasn't fortunate enough to be loved. My new mom thought that if she could criticize and scorn my identity enough, I would be molded into this awesome person (whatever that means) that she wanted me to be, which of course meant I wasn't wanted and valued for who I really was.

My adoptive mom would cut my hair when someone told me I was pretty, would make me scrub the floors with a toothbrush until they were white, would introduce me as Michelle, but introduce her children as her son and daughter. My mom always assumed the worst of me but never asked me who I was, or what I liked. I remember my adoptive mom would hit me, and when I would ask her what I'd done wrong, she would say I looked like I was thinking to do something wrong. As I think of it now, my adoptive mom tried to take away my identity by taking my name. I was born a different name, but she thought it would be best if I change it completely. Back then, I didn't see anything wrong with that, but now, I understand why.

My adoptive dad knew everything that she was doing, but refused to stop it; my worst memory is when I went to him to help me, and all he said was, "I know what she is doing is wrong, but she is my wife, and I'm not going against my wife."

I was constantly whipped, discredited, abused mentally and physically, every day, until the day I chose to leave. The day I left, my mom told me I would not be good enough for anything but lying on my back. She took my head and bashed it against a mirror, shattering it. I made a decision that day. I not only chose to leave my abuser, but I made the decision to somehow live to one day be a voice for those who are undervalued, misunderstood, and neglected.

I lived on the streets, homeless, for two years until I could afford my own place. One night, one of my hardest nights, I thought if I could survive my adoptive mom, I could survive that.

I remember praying and asking God to keep me safe while on these streets, and to guide me into the right direction. Even today, I still pray to God for guidance and allow him to be my light in the darkness.

Through determination, and with God's help, I finally went back to school, obtained my GED, and decided to push through to get my Bachelor of Science in Psychology. It wasn't easy, but it was necessary. I'm currently getting my education as a Clinical Mental Health

Counselor. Then, I will move on to become licensed.

I have walked through many trials in life and learned that walking through is the most important part. I firmly believe that if you want something enough, you can find a way to get it. Having those struggles, and being neglected, with feelings of no hope at times, could've broken me had I stayed in the same cycle. It is getting out of it, walking through it, and grasping who you are because of it, that you can find your purpose around it.

I have times of self-doubt; we all do. During those times, I look back over my life and all that I've been through to remind me where I am going and why I am equipped to get there.

Always remember the cause of other people's actions toward you does not define you, but you can be empowered to reach your goals and follow your dreams, because you walked through it.

So keep dreaming!

Overcome

Michelle Jester

Do you really have to overcome all obstacles? Do you have to climb every mountain and hurdle every boundary to reach the other side?

You absolutely do not.

I don't think I'll ever overcome not seeing my parents more before their deaths. I'll never overcome the selfishness I lived with, thinking they'd always be around or that football practice and cheerleading were more important. While I will never overcome that hurdle, the guilt and pain, I definitely learned from it. Luckily, I don't think on it all the time, but it does hit me every now and then. I have come to learn that chasing one activity after another, or the next big job, is *really* not so important.

I learned to spend time with my husband's grandmother more before she passed. I've learned to appreciate everyone that choses to be a part of my life and let go of the ones that don't. I no longer chase relationships and don't expect anyone to chase me. I learned to simply sit with my husband on the back porch at night, sometimes just enjoying the quiet.

As a small child, quiet was the enemy. Stillness was excruciating.

Growing up, I knew I wasn't smart like my sisters. They both got straight As, and school seemed nearly effortless for them. The one closest to me in age, only thirteen months older, would often stand by the table where I was forced to do my homework, tapping her feet or saying, "Come on, hurry!" Sometimes, when Mom wasn't looking, she'd help me finish early by giving me the answers. Oftentimes, it would've been the only way I could've finished. It wasn't until the second grade that my parents realized something wasn't normal. I remember my mom's frustration at how "hyper" I was all the time. She would say I'd wake up running and didn't stop until I passed out from exhaustion.

I knew there was a problem, too; I simply thought it was me. How else was a child supposed to process something they knew nothing about? Other kids would finish their in-class work and be able to go out to recess much earlier than I was. I would see them out in the schoolyard having fun and laughing, and I was sad. It made it impossible to finish, because all I could think of was finishing early and going outside before the bell rang.

I missed many recesses.

After the diagnosis of Attention Deficient Disorder with hyperactivity, (ADHD now, but that wasn't the term then) which wasn't nearly as common back then as it is now, my mom and dad set out to find a solution. Medicine was the first step, yet a small stint later and it was stopped. Mom told Dad in the kitchen one night that she was taking me off the medicine, because it made me seem like a zombie. She added that my attention hadn't improved, but regressed into nothing.

They tried punishments, rewards, but again nothing worked. No matter the consequence, I simply could not keep my attention focused, and I ended up failing the third grade.

Then, my parents found Mrs. Robinson,

a retired teacher who tutored children with learning issues. Wendy, my sister, sat at the table with us. Mrs. Robinson would look over her homework, but I don't remember her ever really needing a lot of help. Mrs. Robinson was kind, patient, and understanding. Every day before, during, and after tutoring, especially when my attention would drift, Mrs. Robinson had a "mind exercise" that I would have to do. She said it was a tool, not a punishment, but I remember after watching *The Exorcist* as a child thinking, *Did she mean exercise, or exorcise?*

It started out as me putting my hands on the table for a minute and not moving. If I moved within the minute, before the kitchen timer went off, I had to start again. She said during that minute, to simply think. Look inside my mind and see what was in there. I repeated that minute many times, until one day I didn't. Throughout the second round of the third grade, that minute grew to two, three, and then ultimately five. I hated this so much, however, by the end of the year, I was sitting through five full minutes at a time; when my attention would drift away from my task, which wasn't often, five more.

It sounds cruel, and as a child I remember hating it, but I also remember it wasn't punishment ... it was a "tool." I don't advocate this as a solution for parents who have an ADD/ADHD child. I am not your child's parent, nor am I a doctor. I am simply telling my story.

When I no longer needed her and it was to say goodbye, I was sad and scared. She helped me so much, *What would I do without her?* I can still remember Mrs. Robinson's face after all these years.

My grandfather passed away not long after, and the loss hit me hard. My parents brought me to a psychiatrist, and he immediately suggested that they buy me a journal to write my feelings down. I told him about the five-minute-mind-tool, and he told me about keeping lists—list of everything from tasks, to thoughts. It was in that, that my love of writing was born. Writing things down often got them out of my head, so I could focus better. I didn't have to keep up with all the thoughts anymore.

When I tell this story through the years, I often get to this point, and everyone thinks the story is done. They believe that I overcame my obstacle and went on to have straight As. I laugh inside every time, because the reason I would ever tell that story would be to say that, no, often we don't overcome obstacles like that.

I went on to struggle for years. Looking

back at some of my high school report cards, the only good grades I really ever had were in English, Literature, and the occasional fun class like Home Economics. Those classes were interesting. I could keep a list and use the five-minute-mind-tool, and that worked. The rest of my classes were mostly Ds and Fs, and I simply stopped even trying to focus. All through those years, I never stopped writing. I'd write poems, short stories, and novels.

After high school, I worked at McDonald's then Walmart. At the same time, I started at a local center and went through training to be a crisis counselor. It was only on an as-needed basis, so I continued working. I did well at the crisis center, and something clicked for me in that capacity. My parents saw it too and encouraged me to get my associate's degree in counseling. Not long after Larry, my high school sweetheart, and I were married and moved to Virginia where Larry was stationed. There I would eventually start my first business.

Once we moved back to Louisiana and had our daughter, I stayed home with her until she was ready for pre-K. Through the years, I've volunteered with several non-profits, worked for counseling centers, a Christian distributor, publisher, and radio station conglomerate. I've also gotten several other degrees.

I've modified the five-minute-mind-tool; it isn't always five minutes or in the form of me putting my hands on a table, but it still helps keep me focused and to reassess. To think through, then write down.

As it turns out, because of my attention issues, I've learned to improve my results. By simply using the tools I was given, such as pausing, writing, using calendars, and better time management, I am able to organize and prosper. My hyperactivity simply helps me to do more in a shorter amount of time.

Do I get off track? YES! Many times, I can be in the middle of a conversation, think of something I need to do, and I must stop and make a note before I can continue on the conversation. That, or I won't be able to focus on what the person is saying.

Today, I am an author and own several businesses. People often ask me how I am able to do so much. I say my hyperactivity that got on my mom's last nerve, and still gets on my husband's, is actually a good tool itself, when used the right way.

Aside from all the help I've gotten along the way, I've learned God can use us all, even in our struggles.

Despite them.

Because of them.

There are many obstacles you will overcome in life, but for me, it was important to realize I didn't have to overcome them all. Some are obstacles I will always be working to live with. However, God can use us, and all of our obstacles, to our success.[12]

And for the rest of my life, I know I will often find myself using the five-minute-mind-tool.

12. Romans 8:28

Unexpected Blessing

Sharon Carroll Green

When I think about the birth of my first son, I realize how different we handle changes in life depending on our age and stage in life. I was twenty-two when Dalton was born. Young and totally unafraid of what was to come. At that age, I just jumped right in, and learned as I went. Being a mom was lots of fun and extremely rewarding. Dalton and I grew up together somewhat. I made many mistakes, without a doubt, but the love of a child is endless it seems. I could always count on Dalton loving me, even when I didn't love myself.

Which was often.

Sixteen years later, my life was in a self-perpetuated tail spin, totally out of control. I found out I was pregnant with another baby. I hadn't been living a good life; to be honest, quite the opposite. I was totally lost and felt something was missing. I did a lot of drinking, smoking, partying, and had become very promiscuous.

In March of 2009, at the age of thirty-eight, I was pregnant with my second child. That truth alone was difficult, but to add that I didn't really know who the father was made me realize I had plummeted to my lowest. I knew it was between two men, while I was still "legally" married to someone else.

I was terrified and felt like trash. Disgusting.

I had spoken so awfully in the past of women that found themselves in the very same situation I was in. I cried for days without end. I dreaded telling my then sixteen-year-old son the type of life I had been living ... the life that I warned him not to.

I was humiliated.

How did I get here? I thought often enough between the moment I found out to the moment I told Dalton.

When I did find the courage to finally tell him, he simply smiled and said, "Mom, stop crying. God gave you this baby." While I didn't put much thought into that statement at the time, I was so relieved at his acceptance and grace. I had been scared to tell him for fear of judgement or rejection; my son loved me anyway.

A few weeks passed, and I was getting a bit excited about the baby. My obstetrician told me I needed to see a specialist due to my age— just as a precaution to make sure there were no potential birth defects. I agreed, of course. They let me know they would continue to monitor me through the pregnancy since there was a high chance of Down syndrome. I remember thinking, *Yeah okay, that won't happen, but it never hurts to be overcautious.*

During my seventh month, the specialist wanted to do an amniocentesis, and I declined. I'd read up on them, and the chances of premature labor and other potential problems were not worth the risk to me. My obstetrician understood and knew me enough to know that it didn't matter the results, it wouldn't change me having this baby.

Not long after that, I was advised the baby had a blockage in his belly and would have to have immediate surgery after birth to repair it so he would be able to eat without a tube. The doctor also stated that the blockage was one of the characteristics of Down syndrome.

That I should prepare myself.

Panic set in immediately, and I began to blame myself for being such an awful person. I thought possibly God was punishing me through this child. I had awful, shameful thoughts about myself. Still, I was determined to be the best mother this baby could ever have.

So, as life would have it, it moved forward. I began reading up on Down syndrome and trying to prepare myself as much as anyone can.

My oldest son began his junior year in high school, and I was about to have another baby that may or may not have Down syndrome.

The feelings people don't talk about assailed me. I was excited for Dalton, but sad for myself at the same time. My firstborn had grown up way too fast. I missed a lot somewhere inbetween. I was sad and worried. A lot.

One day, out of the blue, Dalton reminded me of a conversation that he and I had before finding out I was pregnant. I had told him that I was going to be all alone when he graduated, and I wish he could stay my baby forever. I wished I had someone that would never leave me. He said God may have answered my prayers by giving me my baby.

I had a very challenging pregnancy. I had gestational diabetes and major amounts of swelling. I had mini seizures and would pass out, not knowing I had a serious heart defect from birth that could've taken my life.

On October 22, 2009, I was induced. I was ready to meet my Dylan. Labor only lasted five hours, but within those hours I had serious breathing issues. My sister kept me focused and calm, and then at 12:36 p.m., my sweet, little man was born.

He had blondish-red hair that stuck straight up. It was so long you could've put it in a ponytail! He was adorable. He was so perfect. He was short, but chunky.

I can honestly say it was love at first sight.

The moment I laid eyes on him, I knew. He had Down syndrome. A million things passed through my mind in those first few seconds, What stood out the most was I had asked God for someone that would never leave me, and here he was.

It was the first time through my entire pregnancy that I realized *God had truly blessed me with this baby.* I knew that everything was going be fine. I had no fear, no doubt, no concern. Simply unconditional love.

I wasn't naïve; I knew there would be challenges starting with surgery looming in the first twenty-four hours to repair the duodenal atresia (blockage between his duodenum and his stomach). Surgery was a huge success, which I knew it would be. After many tests, which I didn't need, it was confirmed he had Down syndrome.

My little superman was born perfectly the way God intended him to be. Three weeks later, (and seventeen years later to the day after my first son came home) my second one came home from the hospital to a house full of people that had been waiting to hold him since he was born.

Fast forward two more years to me finding out that I had a birth defect, hypertrophic-cardiomyopathy. That should've caused my death in giving birth to Dalton and Dylan, and I began to see The Lord's plan. I now have a pacemaker and a defibrillator. By all accounts, I shouldn't be alive today.

By most accounts, neither should Dylan.

Yet, God has bigger plans.

Dalton is now twenty-seven, has a wife, and has given me two beautiful grandbabies. Dalton

Jr (Boogie) is six years old and Charli Rae is three. Dylan is now ten. He is fairly healthy and does not have many health issues.

I know God used Dylan to save my life. I was on a path of self-destruction, with no hope, alone with deep feelings of looming abandonment. I felt thoroughly unworthy.

I've learned to let God lead my footsteps.

I learned that God's blessings for us may not always seem like blessings at first. I have to trust.

I also learned not to judge the way other people live. Judging others removes love, replacing it with rejection and rules. When I told Dalton about my pregnancy almost eleven years ago, worried he would judge me as I had judged many others, he accepted me instead. He showed me a true grace I had never known before.

Imagine the grace God has.

A Life Like Nana and Woo

Marcie Klock

When my brother and I were young, we spent a lot of time with our Nana and Wo. They were really our great aunt and uncle, but felt like more of a combination of grandparents and parents.

Nana was a fairly tall woman. She was 5'10", dark brown hair, eyes that seemed to change color, kind of fluffy build, but eventually turned slightly frail and fragile in her later years. Wo stood about 6'4", beautiful blue eyes, slightly light-colored hair. slender, but fit. They were perfect for each other. Nana and Wo were my examples of the fairy tale love story we all see in the books and hope to have. No book matches what these two shared.

Nana and Wo had rules, much like our Uncle Charles and Aunt Glenna.

Nana and Wo woke every morning praying, on their knees together, holding hands in their bedroom.

They would make their coffee and have Bible study together, and then their day would begin with their routines. They ended each night on their knees at bedtime, holding hands, praying together. For whatever reason, as a little girl, I always cried during their prayer time. Always. Even as a teen, I still cried. I didn't know then, but I now know, those tears were Holy Spirit tears, because their prayers were big, bold, and all heart. No one came close to praying like Nana and Wo. Coming in a close second place would be our Uncle Charles and Aunt Glenna.

A lot of good things happened around Nana and Wo's table. That table is so significant.

My Nana knew the Bible inside and out. People from their church would call my Nana with problems and in need for prayer, and my Nana would resort to scripture, over and over.

She'd pull her Bible out and read the scripture that was on her heart for whatever obstacle or challenge that person on the other end of the phone was facing.

I say all of this to stress that I have seen amazing relationships and marriages based on faith, God, and love that were enormous influences to me during my childhood, and those that were the very best examples I could have had—even hoped for.

Nana and Wo were not just amazing human beings who gave us a great life, an amazingly beautiful and pristinely clean place to stay, but they loved us with all of their hearts. They wanted the best for us, and they wanted God and faith to be the center of our life.

We would eventually lose both Nana and Wo due to different types of cancer, but we had them for a time in our life that was so instrumental to the foundation of my brother and me. Nana and Wo wanted kids, but they could never have them. We lost Wo first, and Nana would be a widow for years, until she passed.

Before bedtime, Wo always took his watch off as he did his night-time bathroom routine of washing his face, brushing his teeth, his watch always laid on the vanity in the bathroom on his side, above the sink, and of course Nana had her own side with her stuff. When Wo passed away, the battery died in his watch the very minute he took his last breath. His watch laid on that vanity up until my Nana, many years later, would move out of the house they had built and shared together for most of their marriage.

I longed to be like Nana later in life. As a child, I sometimes thought she was tough, over the top with her love for the Lord, but now I see why, and it all makes perfect sense to me. The truth is, her love was spot on for the Lord and how we are all supposed to be living.

I always dreamed to be like Nana, and I always dreamed I'd find my Wo. For all the reasons that I have mentioned earlier. It would take me hardship, pain, and years to find my Wo, but I finally did.

To top it off, the other night, I received a message from my brother who doesn't throw out compliments often. He said, "I am so proud of the woman you have become. Nana would be, too." I will cherish this compliment forever, because as you can see, Nana was such a special lady to me.

I wish I still had her today.

It took me so much to get here. So much hardship and pain.

It's rare to not think of Nana and Wo, especially where I am right now in life. I often think of the smell of their home; it had a distinct smell and was so perfect. I don't know if timbers, woodburning fire, and chestnuts will sum it up, but that's what it smelled like. In the colder times of the year, they typically had a fire burning.

I think of coffee time with Nana. Her coffee was the best, along with her bread and food. She was the best cook. Anything she fixed was unreal.

If you still have your Nana or Wo, go visit. Give them a call. Tell them you love them and how much they mean to you. Life is unpredictable and mortality is tough. Cherish the time while you have it. Let those you have with you now, today, know how much they mean to you. It is never too late to express how much you love someone, until they are gone.

Sit at their table with them; love on them.

Life is a gift. Wake up every day and realize that.[13]

13. Psalm 90:12

The Great Mother

Joy Morrow-Holden

I always thought I would be a great mother. I have a fantastic mother, and I loved kids. I considered myself patient, sweet, maternal, and intelligent. I had worked with children on and off for years, and was pretty good at it. I didn't lose my temper. I was calm handling conflict. I naturally expected these qualities would transfer into idyllic motherhood.

Then, I had my son, and he taught me more about myself than I could've ever imagined.

Those thoughts of great motherhood went

out the window when my oldest son reached about two-and-a-half years old. He had a knack for screaming inconsolably; screaming at me through tears, or just screaming at me in anger. He would slam his doors and yell as loud as he could, for as long as he could. He was passionate and intense, and our power struggles were epic.

To my surprise, I did not handle it calmly. To my surprise, a rage burst out of me. An anger I had never felt before rose up in me and forced itself out. I yelled back. I was harsh. Then, I would walk away.

Once I had some space, I composed myself, hugged him, and we made up. I apologized for losing my temper. He was a fierce and determined little boy, and I was discovering a suppressed anger that was unknown to me. This combination led to tumultuous and difficult moments.

Many of them.

One still is on replay in my mind and in my heart. One morning, on the way to school in the car, something had set him off. He was almost four at the time. I was dropping off his brother at the nursery when he started throwing a fit. Tears spurted out of his eyes, his little face was red, and his voice was loud. I could not calm him down. I tried whispering. I tried comforting. I tried yelling back. I tried spanking him. I eventually got him to a teacher and just asked for her help.

Then, I went into a bathroom and cried.

I cried, because I couldn't mother him the way he needed. I cried, because my feelings were hurt. I cried, because of insecurity. But most of all, I cried because of shame. I was so ashamed of my weakness and anger. I wanted to hide in that bathroom the entire day. After desperate sobs and deep sighs, I finally wiped my tears and walked to class to teach someone else's children.

How could this be me? I was the happy one, the friendly one, the sweet one.

Where was this madness coming from, and why was I directing it toward my most prized jewel?

See, I had prayed for him. I had longed for him. After losing our first to a miscarriage, I was so deeply thankful for him.

Was I profoundly screwing him up?

Did my temper cause irreparable damage?

What was wrong with me?

These were the questions I constantly asked myself. Only, I didn't have any answers.

Thankfully, over time, he developed more

communication skills to express his intense emotions, and I learned to respond differently. We both had been locked in a power struggle for years. I wanted to prove that I was the dominant one, and so did he. I realized that our pattern was not how he would grow and develop into a compassionate, kind, and balanced person.

Finally, I decided to overcome the shame with vulnerability. I confessed all of this internal and external conflict to a friend one afternoon. I reached out for empathy, but I really expected condemnation. The empathy came and showered over me. In that moment, I decided to overcome the anger and shame with love.

I will love him harder.

I will hug him spontaneously.

I will pick him up just to hear him laugh.

I will pull him on my lap and hold him, just because.

We will cuddle on the couch.

I will read to him often.

I will hand him praises, like he hands me flowers.

I will treasure his drawings, his words, his ideas, his LEGO creations, and his crazy inventions.

I will exalt every little moment he takes my

hand.

He will know he is loved and valued.

I now refuse to give into the shame. I am doing the hard work of discovery and healing on the inside, and I am doing the great work of loving him extra hard on the outside.

I let go of the notions of what a great mother I thought I'd be, to learn what being a great mother really is.

Give Yourself a Break

Michelle Jester

Often we are running around trying to be super human, because we feel we must. Our responsibilities are never-ending. From running errands, to cleaning and cooking, to basic personal hygiene, it all takes a toll on our bottom line: time. That's not to mention work and taking care of the other humans and animals in our lives.

With juggling everything, it's easy to fall into guilt when things slip through the cracks. However, life will go on. Mistakes happen.

My kids are grown now, but when they were younger, we were lucky sometimes if we made it home in time to eat the hamburgers we rushed through the drive-thru to get, before we had to head back out the door for one practice or another.

Here's the good news: we all survived the mistakes and I learned better time management in the process. I keep a schedule that is made weeks, if not months, ahead of time, and it stays pretty packed. However, I know not everything is going to go according to the plan. I also learned that's okay.

First, I stopped beating myself up about the things I couldn't control. Flat tire? Oh well, theatre practice will have to do without one of the kids tonight.

I had to stop getting frustrated with situations that were out of my control.

Second, I started reassessing the things I could change. Us running late in the morning because that extra fifteen minutes of ironing was disturbing my flow, was an easy fix. I bought wrinkle spray and quickly found that a few spritz on my clothes and a few minutes in the dryer while I put on my makeup did wonders!

I had to learn to better manage the things

that were in my control.

Last, I learned to give myself a break. Not to beat myself up over all the mistakes: being late, missed family dinners, or forgotten field trips. I can only do so much, and accepting that was the key.

I had to forgive myself for my misgivings and accept that I can't do it all.

Release things you can't control, try to better manage what you can, and give yourself a break on all the other things. Maintaining a balance mentally is far more important to you and your family than making it to every practice on time.

Out With the Old, In With the New

Nicole Brice

After college, I was working for a local fast-food restaurant as a manager but was growing tired of the job itself, because, to be honest, I had a new college degree, and I wanted to explore my other options. This exploration led me to a job at a national rental car company, where I was hired as a station manager at one of their airport locations. I had managed personnel in the quick service restaurant industry, but never in such a corporate setting. This job taught me something I needed: new managerial skills. It was a great learning experience, but eventually, I was offered my dream job, and so I said my goodbyes to my co-workers and off I went again.

In October of 2006, I was called to submit my résumé for a marketing position with the local franchisee office of the fast-food restaurant chain I had previously worked for. This local management company had owned and operated the restaurant where I had worked for so long, so I was beyond stoked to continue working for a company that treated me well and that I had longevity with. After a few weeks of anxiously waiting for a phone call letting me know whether I landed the position, and a subsequent interview, I finally received a call from my soon-to-be boss letting me know that they were going to make me an offer. Yes!

I became the Marketing Merchandising Manager for that franchisee, which had over fifty restaurants. I was required to keep up with all promotional materials in the restaurants, as well as work special events and be a "face" for the company. It was hard work, but I knew that if the leadership saw what a hard worker I was that eventually I would be rewarded with either more work or a promotion. From 2006 until early 2011, I plugged away at my job. I never missed a beat. I was on a path to success, and I was determined to not stop until I got there.

In the fall of 2010, all office staff were asked to come into the training room one afternoon for a last-minute meeting. We all were wondering what was happening, and we waited. The owners told us that the company was splitting into two different companies and that the staff would be evenly distributed between them, but that no one would lose their job. I was apprehensive at first about the BIG change, but I was looking forward to the challenge and wondered what was planned for me and my career.

Later that week, one of the owners called me into his office to let me know that he was taking me with him and in April 2011 I was promoted to Brand Manager over thirty-one restaurants in two states with my new company. It was finally my time to shine and show them what I could do. I knew I had something to prove, and I wanted to prove that I was worthy of my new position.

From 2011 until 2016, I worked as Brand Manager for my company. I traveled all over. I did TV and radio interviews. I organized and planned special events and grand openings. I was working even when I was "off." I did feel as though there was nowhere else to move upward and wanted more at times.

In March 2016, I went on several interviews for a Quality Service Restaurant Industry competitor in hopes of landing a corporate marketing position with this new company. If I landed this job, I could finally break free, start fresh, and prove myself creatively as an asset in the marketing world. I was flown to the company headquarters, and after several months of back-and-forth emails, and numerous interviews, I received the phone call I had been waiting for. The competitor wanted me, and they offered me more benefits and pay. My mind was made up instantly. I wanted this job. This was it. This was my time. Sure, I would have to drive more, and the idea of venturing out into new territory scared the living daylights out of me, but I felt that I needed to grow. I was only growing stagnant where I was. And if I was fully honest, I was also growing more and more undervalued. We all experience that at points in our careers, because it's business to businesses, but personal to us.

I turned in my resignation upon accepting the new position, but I hadn't signed their employment contract just yet, so it wasn't set in stone. Upon turning in my resignation, everyone was in shock. The owner couldn't believe it. He even told me he was "shook" by my decision. The next few weeks were met with numerous meetings with the owner and eventually, he offered for me to stay by matching the pay and benefits offered to me by the competitor, but I was told it would come in two phases. I had very high respect for this man, and still do, so I trusted and believed that I would receive everything promised that day. I had a tough decision to make. Should I stay where I was unhappy but "secure," or should I dive right in and go for the new job that had solid track record of advancement, but required change? Ultimately, I decided to stay, which turned out to be the wrong decision in the long run.

In the coming months, then years, when the owner did not hold true to his promises, including the second phase of my pay increase, I felt utterly betrayed. I ran the gambit of emotion from disappointed to flat out resentment for being taken advantage of. Like many who've been through the same situation, I was a fool! My husband kept nudging me to leave and did not think I would ever see any of the promises come to fruition. I kept telling him how loyal the owner was to me, as I was to him. My husband simply didn't understand. I made excuse after excuse for my boss's inaction, or action by default. I kept holding out hope that I would get all that was promised to me.

Unfortunately, I never did.

After my son was diagnosed with Autism in May 2017, my world was turned upside down. (There I was ... I was pregnant at the time with my daughter and going through a tough pregnancy. Not to mention on top of being involved in a motor vehicle accident while pregnant with her, which later turned into bed rest for me during the last month of my pregnancy, where I was told sneezing wrong could cause me to go into labor. During that last month, though, while in bed, I wanted to do my full job with the exception of the driving part. I saw no need to stop that type of work simply because I was in bed. I was amazed at how much I could get accomplished while not physically able to be at the brick and mortar location.

Throughout this entire time, the owner kept complimenting me and saying that no matter what, he wanted me back when I was ready. My future was uncertain due to my son and his numerous therapies requiring transportation by one of us, but just knowing that I was thought so highly of made me happy, and I was determined to get back to my job, sooner rather than later, because the job was mine, and I knew I deserved the promises I'd been given.

Nearly a year-and-a-half later, in August 2019 I was still working from home as the Marketing Director, and still handling up on my business, working extra hours to meet the needs of the company. I got an email from the owner requesting to meet for our quarterly marketing meeting. Once I got there for the meeting, the receptionist told me to "go check my box," which I realized later was a polite way of saying, "Girl, I didn't want to be the one to tell you." I went to my box, only to discover that my name plate had been replaced with a new name. I found mine a few rows below along with other supervisors.

My heart sank. That is how I was told that I'd been demoted.

I got to the meeting, and the owner was his usual, jovial self. So, I relaxed a bit. There was obviously a mistake somewhere. He started by giving me a list of normal marketing tasks he needed completed and then ... *the bombshell.*

"We've hired someone for marketing," he said. "Your role will change."

As he was talking, I was in shock. I was unable to process a thought, much less words.

I felt blindsided, and my entire insides were vibrating. He and I agreed I would still work from home, and I would have a new title. I was on the verge of tears.

The drive home was brutal. I've never cried so hard in my entire life. I was mourning.

Mourning the loss of a department I had single-handedly built by myself.

Mourning the death of my career.

Mourning the trust I had in a man that had built me up so much to blindside me like that.

For the next few months, I continued working from home, but my drive to work for the company just wasn't there anymore. I was rejected, and rejection hurts. Not to mention, my future with the company was now uncertain. I no longer felt safe, which was the reason I had stayed.

After several months of poor treatment, which I suspected was intentional to get me to do just as I had, I finally sent in a formal resignation. I thought that was it, and I was now free to explore new options. My husband was right, and I hated that, too. He predicted that my boss would make one last ditch effort at keeping me, which he did, but it wasn't the same as before. This time, I saw him differently. He was cold, calloused, and I realized he only wanted to keep me so I could "train" the new director. After listening to his speech, I calmly told him I still intended to resign. He was shocked.

Instead of feeling victorious, I left feeling even more defeated. I was down. So down that I thought I'd never stop crying. I missed so much in my personal life, working so hard to build that company, and was left feeling I was leaving with little reward to show for it.

Through that, God sent two great women, to lift me up, dust me off, dry my tears ... and it brought me back to life. One I call my "wifey" as a joke, however she is my emotional equal, my twin. The other is a phenomenal powerhouse in business and a real beauty in her personal life. Both of these women lifted me in different ways.

If it wasn't for these women, I worry that it would've taken much longer to recover from such a huge rejection. It's amazing what the power of female friendship can do, and I am forever grateful for their love and friendship.

Here I am at forty, starting over. I'm not only okay with it, I'm excited. I have a supportive husband, and I feel alive for the first time in a while. I'm ready to conquer!

I realize my feelings of betrayal were due to

how much I put into that business, and how high I regarded the owner of it. However, I left with much more than I went into it with, and they were left the same way. That is what matters now, looking back.

I am on to my new adventure, one that all of my hard work will reap benefits for me directly. I have started my own consulting firm, and with God's help, I find that my life grows fuller by the day.

My Best Defense Isn't Me

Marcie Klock

The morning had been off to a wonderful start. Then one disagreement later, and I just needed to pick up the phone and call one of my soul sisters. I am fortunate to have a couple of people in my life that I can always count on and turn to for prayer and support. Through my sisterhood and friendship with one of them, I know I can be one hundred percent vulnerable and not feel judged, shamed, or negated.

"Can you just pray with me?" I can call and ask. Most of the time I am specific with telling her what I am walking through, but there have been those times where I've simply said, "I need your voice and prayer." Her voice always brings me so much comfort, peace, and a place of love.

You hear female pastors or leaders who talk about the ladies they admire, and they just want to sit at their feet and learn from them. Michelle is that to me. In all that she has been up against in life, she's someone I see that has true obedience and love for the Lord. I admire her, but more importantly, I trust her.

Sometimes, I get so busy moving at a fast pace that I tend to forget to stop and ask myself, *Am I doing what God has called me to do?*

As I talked my frustrations out with her, told her how in my deep aggravation during the disagreement went, I found myself beginning to rehearse my replies. I was thinking preemptively, *Oh, I am going to say this, and they will reply with this, and then that is when I will tell them this*—She gently reminded me in that moment that I am not supposed to keep the argument going according to scripture. She explained the verse in the Bible.

In that moment, I realized no matter how much I feel nagged or irritated, I am not supposed to defend myself and have this immediate need to verbally punch back.[14]

This has been hard for me for so many reasons. I realized during the conversation, that this had been a stronghold of mine. My friend gently nudged me that day to just go and be with God. She said, "No matter what you feel, or how hurt you are, simply show that person love. Don't punch back."

While I suppose it is human nature for us to want to defend ourselves when we feel we are being wronged or insulted, I realized that during my life, the need to argue had never actually helped me. It never brought me fruitful endings to an argument or misunderstanding.[15] My counter punches never produced joy or happiness. It more than likely caused an argument or disagreement to escalate. This conversation and situation led me to the scripture of the quarrelsome wife in Proverbs.[16] For whatever reason, that day, this is where the Lord took me. A hardened heart isn't something Godly or sent by God. The more I continue to examine myself, I realize I want to strive to be the best version of myself I can be.

While God has made me unique in my own ways, I realize that fighting the need to defend myself and verbally punch back is going to require a lot of discipline and prayer. The enemy knows us each well, and he has tools in

197

his belt tucked aside to throw at us, so we must stay aware. He will always use his tactics.

I know, for me, it is so important in those types of moments of weakness to pause before I speak and seek God, His presence, peace, and love. I notice when I am exhausted, my responses and reactions can be quick and defensive. Just because I am over-worked, over-committed, or feel under-appreciated, doesn't give me the excuse to lash out and react negatively. I won't always get it right, but I will always continue to work on it.

That day, I learned something about myself, and even though my husband has pointed it out, it took a completely different scenario to make me see it.

My come backs and counter punches are not gifts from God.

Exactly opposite.

It shows a lack of patience ... and to be honest, a lack of faith, in not waiting and allowing God to defend me.

Because I know, without a doubt, my best defense isn't me.

14. 1 Peter 2:23
15. Proverbs 15:18
16. Proverbs 27:15-16

Our Hearts

Kristi Williams Fontenot

Diamonds are forever!

We have all heard that saying before, especially when it comes attached to an engagement. Have you ever wondered where diamonds come from or how diamonds are made? Diamonds are formed from tiny carbon deposits deep within the earth that, when placed under heat and the pressure of the earth's gravity, form a rough diamond. When they are pulled from the earth you probably would not even think they were of value, because from the outside they look more like an old, dirty rock. But on the inside, is a beauty that can only be called a diamond. As light hits the diamond, it begins to shine as the light is reflected off it. The more light a diamond gets, the more the diamond will sparkle. To this day, diamonds are still one of the most beautiful, reflective, and tough stones earth has ever given us.

When I think about how a diamond forms, I cannot help but relate that to what life looks like for us as Christians. Before we begin our walk with Christ from the inside, our hearts are not a thing of beauty. As a matter of fact, our hearts may be carrying around extra baggage that could even harden our hearts. As a new Christian, a transformation begins in our hearts the day we accept Christ as our savior. It is not something that happens overnight, but instead is a work-in-progress.

During that process, we may even go through moments or seasons where it feels like life is squeezing us. Maybe you feel like your four walls are closing in on you, and the pressures of life feel too hard to handle.

I have been there!

Sometimes, I want nothing more than to wave my white flag and surrender to life. Recently, I had one of those days. We own a small mom and pop restaurant. Most people see the front side of a restaurant. It's calm; food comes from the kitchen plated and brought to your table. People wait patiently for their orders to go. But what you do not see is the craziness of the kitchen. I am sure you have heard that old saying *if you can't take the heat stay out of the kitchen.* Well in our business, it's so true. To say the kitchen is HOT in a restaurant in south Louisiana would be an understatement most days. It is not just the cooking that makes a kitchen hot. It is the busyness and mess of the kitchen that makes it so hot. The amount of people in the kitchen to make it operate properly that makes the kitchen hot. And ultimately it is the stress in the kitchen that makes it hot, hot, hot!

From the outside, you would not even know that in the heart of that restaurant it is truly a hot mess. We are the same way. From the outside, we may look fine. We may put on a show of acting like all is fine, but inside we feel the pressure of life closing in on us. As those pressures build up, it has a way of revealing what is inside our hearts.

It was one of those days that we were shorthanded from the start. In the restaurant business, being shorthanded just means that the boss works even harder than normal, because they get to cover two positions instead of one.

YAY for me being the boss!

It is hard to start your day off feeling behind from the moment you walk in the door. By nine in the morning, our food delivery service iPad was going off with a future order that needed to be delivered for noon. As I accepted the order, I noticed it had something on the ticket that we did not cook that day. I could either reject the order, and potentially make the customer unhappy, or I could cook what they were asking for. They were feeding at least ten people, so I assumed it was important and made the choice to accept the order and cook what they needed. After all we are in the business to make the customer happy.

In our restaurant, we cook in bulk in the morning for our lunch crowd and any catering orders. Then we re-access the kitchen after lunch and cook for the evening. By nine we are nearly done cooking, so I had no choice but to get the stove going again to fulfill the order. While cooking, I realized the salad that had just come in that morning from my vendor was no good, so I left the stove going for my employees to watch and ran to the store to get fresh salad for the day. When I returned from the store, the phone was ringing, and on the other end was a friend's mother looking for enough food for seventy-five people. She asked me if it was too late to get it for early afternoon, and of course I said that was no problem at all. At that point, I was sure I sounded wild ... but just wait, it gets wilder. I got off the phone, and quickly lit the fire under a few of our big pots to start re-cooking to ensure we had enough for the seventy-five, plus enough for our lunch rush.

By that time, it was nearly time to turn the open signs on for our lunch crowd, and then I noticed our three-compartment sink was nearly flooding the kitchen. I turned the water off and began mopping the water that was creeping its way across the floors. I could feel the anxiety and stress swelling up inside me.

I mean, who has time to deal with a flooding kitchen and fix the sink while trying to take care of the normal business for the day, the unexpectedly added business for the day, all while being shorthanded?

It is in moments like these that those around us see what we are truly made of on the inside. Are we going to let our circumstances dictate our behavior, or are we going to let our heart dictate our behavior?[17] It was one of those moments where I could definitely say that the kitchen was too "hot," but one way or another, I was not going to let it get the best of me. I knew the devil was going to win, only if I allowed him to. So right then and there in the middle of my wet mopping I declared out loud … "Not today devil! My kitchen may be upside down, and you may be trying to get the best of me today, but I am not going to let you win!"

I had a choice to make in that moment.

I could either let the devil win by getting angry and frustrated, or I could let God win by letting Him control the way my heart felt.[18]

I do not know about you, but I do not want anyone to think for one second that I sound like a fool. On the contrary, self-control is a sign to others that we have the fruit of the Holy Spirit living within us. How we react to situations that are out of our control should always be a reflection of our relationship with Jesus Christ.

The thing is, as the pressure gets too hot, oftentimes that's when the true spiritual transformation within us begins. When we turn to God in the difficult times, *He* will do amazing things in our hearts as we listen to Him for guidance and strength.[19] There are even times where God allows us to walk through and experience things in our life so that when we turn to Him, He can begin to mold us into the person He is creating us to be. Our hearts will undergo a transformation just like the diamond did when the heat and pressure were applied.

God wants nothing more than for our hearts to shine with His love and glory. The beauty that a diamond exemplifies is the same beauty God wants for us. The beauty that can only come from a heart that is completely surrendered to Him.

17. Proverbs 4:23
18. Proverbs 29:11
19. Ezekiel 36:26

Power of the Tongue

Sara Simoneaux

What is your trigger word?
What does that word mean to you?
To your child?
To your niece or nephew?
To your student, friend, or neighbor?
Stupid.
Ugly.
Fat.
Skinny.
Bad.
Poor.

Trashy.

Conceited.

Slut.

Tease.

Ignorant.

Filthy.

Annoying.

Plain.

Obnoxious.

Disgusting.

Worthless.

So many words that, in passing, may seem insignificant, but to someone they are defining. They are everything.

Often, they are the only thing.

How aware are you of the impact your words have on others? How carefully do you censor yourself?

There are so many things we do and say in front of others, especially young children, that we think are harmless. When in reality it may define them for years.

In children, we think that they aren't listening. We think that they don't understand. The unfortunate reality is that very often they are listening, but they understand words differently than we do. They are literal. In a time when they are searching for approval and love, those words can be their anchor in their own self-discovery. We adults already know the impact, because each of us has words that were embedded in us from somewhere throughout our lives. Too loud, too quiet, too fat, too skinny. They impact us long after our childhoods. A complex has taken root, and the damage has been done.

It can take years to dig through those strongholds. Even as adults, when we can recognize that some of those words weren't said to intentionally hurt us, they are still there.

Our kids are suffering today in ways kids never have before. The internet is such an influence in their lives. Anyone and everyone has become the co-parent and the encyclopedia all-in-one. Adolescent anxiety and depression are at an all-time high, and we don't even stop to consider how we've gotten here. Our kids are growing up in a society where *Teen Moms* and *The Kardashians* equate to celebrity and success.

Do you know who it is that your child idolizes?

Do you know what they're streaming once you've gone to sleep?

There is a recurring void in people's lives, young ones especially, that is being filled by others, as well as yourself.

What are those voids being filled with?

We can't monitor everything our children are exposed to, and we surely can't fill in voids for adults, but we can watch our words. We can pour good, solid, confidence-building words into those around us. That doesn't mean we can't correct others. It means we can affirm, even in correction, by loving people honestly.[20]

When we all need to keep in mind that the power of life and death are literally in the words we speak, and that we will live by the words we choose, we will better watch what we pour out.[21]

Practice sowing good, positive words in the world around you. You'll find that your fruit will grow sweeter, your children more empowered, and you will reap the rewards of life more abundantly.

20. Proverbs 27:6
21. Proverbs 18:21

Second Chances

Brandi LeBlanc

Once upon a time, there was this girl who had some really big dreams. A dream of being "known." Not just known, but worth knowing. A dream of being on the big screen. She had dreams of not only of making a difference in her own small town life, but making a difference in the lives of other people. She knew she was a nobody and thought often, *Who am I to do such things?* As a little girl going through school, she was bullied. She was made fun of, found herself as the brunt of kids' jokes, was always picked last, and was always told, even by her own mother, that she would never amount to anything. She grew up with that in the back of her mind ... but still, she never lost hold of that dream.

That little girl was me.

I married young. One month out of high school, I was mother to a six-month-old baby. By the age of twenty-four, I had four children with my first husband. After divorcing him at the age of twenty-five, I fell in love with my best friend's brother. He had a hold on my heart that no other person ever had before ... but it was toxic to my soul.

During that marriage, it broke me. He broke me. But I couldn't get away. I tried several times, but he always drew me back in. There were so many times he'd promise that he would never do it again, but he broke that promise as soon as he got me back home.

I couldn't decide if it was true love, or if it was an obsession. I had no job, no vehicle, no independence. He made sure he tore me down, mentally and physically. He beat me to the point of breaking bones. Among some of the attacks, he ran me over with his truck, held me at gun point, and attempted to drown me in a sink while I was pregnant with his child.

He constantly told me that I would never amount to anything and would never make it on my own. Always told me that I wasn't good enough and never would be … and I believed him. Every single word. I felt my dreams being crushed with the brunt of every punch, every derogatory comment made to me. I had every piece of me broken. At one point, seeing no other way out, I tried to kill myself. During that same period, I lost custody of four of my five children, the four from my previous marriage. I lost my entire self-worth, and the only thing that kept me going was the child I shared with him. I had to protect her.

In 2011, I was rescued and my life transformed. I always knew of Him, but never really "knew" Him. It wasn't until then that I found a relationship with God, and He spoke to me, that I truly believed that the life I had been leading was not the end for me. This was not the purpose He had for me, but it was for His purpose and plan that I had to endure and help others.

After a year of prayer and having God reveal to me that He had bigger plans, He provided me a way to escape, and a way to allow Him to build me up into the woman He wanted me to be.

God told me that I was worthy and that He would prove it to me and help me find my purpose. With him, I found myself and the strength within me. With God, I found my identity. He made me worthy of "being known." He made me a warrior. Through His faithfulness to me, my faith grew in Him. I knew that I could do anything that I put my mind to and that He would be with me through it all. He promised me, and I believed Him. He wanted my testimony to be one of redemption, of power, and of purpose.

I became planted in a church and found that God repeatedly placed me in leadership roles, helping other women find their strength, mentally and spiritually. Not only was I helping other women who were in my exact previous predicament, He placed me in roles helping drug addicts, like my ex-husband, find their own strength and faith in God to help them battle the chains of addiction. Block-by-block God built me from a physically and mentally broken woman, who had lost four of her five children and her entire self-worth, to being a mentor who helps to build up other people, including ones like my abusive ex-husband.

It wasn't easy. Many times God would place

me in someone's path, and the self-doubt would try to creep back in, but all I had to do was to remind myself who God was in me.

One day in 2014, though I wasn't even looking for a romantic relationship at the time, I met a man at the church that I was attending and immediately felt drawn to him. During the time of our courting, he took me into a gym and started showing me the ropes. He helped me find my physical strength and encouraged me, physically and spiritually. He helped me see that not only was I a warrior on the inside, but that I was a warrior physically as well. He supported me and helped me become the strongest woman I had ever been ... physically and spiritually.

After two years, he helped me transform my body in ways that I never thought was possible. In 2016, I became an athlete competing in local bodybuilding shows as a Women's Bodybuilder, winning several national titles, awards, and even earned my pro-card status as a Professional Women's Bodybuilder.

All in my first year of competing.

I quickly became a highly-respected, well-known personal trainer on a mission to help others transform.

During my training and preparation

for these shows, I got my certification as a personal trainer. At that time, God spoke into me that this is what He was preparing me for: to help empower other women, of all shapes, sizes, ages, and races, to find strength within themselves to reach goals that they never thought was possible.

After training in commercial gyms for only three years, my clientele was big enough, and loyal enough, to open my own private training studio, Barbelle Beauty Fitness. Within five years, God had helped me build a community of women that shared the same goals, needed the same strengthening, and a safe, nonjudgmental place to build themselves up. He spoke to me that this place should be one of power ... His power, and that I should help these women find their worth and strength beyond their wildest imaginations. I am in awe that He chose me to help them tap into it.

I found a passion to help other women find their strength. And in that, I found my purpose.

All that I had been through, all of the hurt and abuse were not caused for purpose, but God is using them for it. The life of turmoil will not be wasted. My passion, my purpose, and my assignment in life became to share exactly what God had brought through, while helping women physically meet their goals.

There is no other explanation for my rapid success, except that this growth is the supernatural hand of God. He is on my business, because my purpose is in going about His business. My influence can only have come from one source, and that source is God.

My training studio, Barbelle Beauty Fitness, is not just about physical strength and weight loss. God has helped me build an empire of powerful women who were once torn down and broken because of their physical appearances and emotional instabilities due to mental and physical abuse. Women who needed to find a balance in doing for their family, but also learning how to make themselves a priority in order to be healthy enough to care for their families as needed.

I even have some of their husbands enrolled into a men's group that I now run, encouraging them to be leaders of their home, spiritually, mentally, and physically and to be an example to their children of a strong leader. This has become my passion more than my profession, because I know that this is the calling of my life.

Because the studio space that I moved into two years ago was bursting at the seams, my husband and I just signed on a new, larger building to continue God's vision for us.

In 2020, I was named Best Trainer in our area, as well as the Best Fitness Center/Gym, topping out some of the big-time, commercial gyms. I currently write a fitness column for a local magazine, *Ascension Magazine*, and am a contributor to a statewide lifestyle publication, *Modern Grace magazine*. Of course, as always with God, my story doesn't end there.

After twelve years of standing on the promises of God, I was finally awarded 50/50 custody of the children that I had lost while I was in the deepest despair of my life.

No matter where you are in life, or what situation has you held captive, there is hope in your situation. His name is Jesus. Even a broken, torn-down, small-town, picked-on-all-her-life girl who had a silly dream of "being known." That girl learned, with Him all things are possible.[22]

No matter how bad things are, and no matter what man says about you, God's purpose for you will always triumph.[23] He is not only the God of second chances, but He is the God of rebirth and restoration.

22. Matthew 19:26
23. Luke 1:45

Adversary or Ally

Michelle Jester

Just after we'd bought our first house in Virginia, I was set to speak at a women's conference. I had a radio campaign that gifted Valentine's Day photography and makeover packages through my business running on the radio for four weeks prior, and it brought me to the attention of one of the conference directors. While the conference was small, I was especially excited, because it was the first one I'd been asked to contribute to that wasn't coordinated through one of the local churches or for military dependents.

I worked on my speech all week. It's funny to remember how important I felt having a computer. Larry bought it from a friend, and I used it often. Matter of fact, I started *The Funeral Flower*, my first published novel, on that very computer. Anyway, with Larry's mean editing skills, we honed the speech until it was perfect. I printed two copies on our continuous form paper printer, put them in my portfolio and safely tucked the portfolio away in my satchel.

Larry had just bought me the satchel so I would look, and feel, professional. He believes in having quality accessories, and he is right. That one satchel carried me through my first company and boosted my confidence professionally.

The day finally arrived. Larry was deployed, and I had one of my best friends watching our son. I was ecstatic! I arrived at the designated time and was taken to a holding room with the other speakers. I mingled, as usual, but the atmosphere was definitely different. Making my rounds through the tight space to meet all the other women and engage was hard enough in such a small area, but to say the mood was tense would be an understatement.

Soon, a man came to usher us to the main building. He warned us that it was pouring down rain and handed us umbrellas to share. He also said we could leave any valuables, such as purses, because the door would be locked until the end of the day. I immediately thought of my satchel, the new one Larry bought me. I didn't want it to get rained on, so I eased my portfolio out of it and left it sitting safely on a chair.

Not long after, I was scooting through the rain with my umbrella partner in a line of women.

And I started giggling.

I can't help it, I always giggle when I'm running through the rain, and I have no idea why. I assume, because it makes me feel like a child, but again, I really can't pinpoint it. My daughter says it's because my spirit animal is a little yellow duckie. I honestly can't disagree.

Anyway, there I was giggling, running through the rain, and I glanced over at my umbrella partner. She was looking at me like I had sprouted an extra head, which quickly caused me stop giggling. I remember feeling the odd sense of extreme insecurity. The last time I'd felt it was right after we had Jaymes-Irish, years before. Then, as I'm known to do, I tripped slightly (anyone who knows me well enough knows I'm a total klutz) and my portfolio went flying out of my hands ... into a deep puddle of water.

By the time we made it to the main holding area and I opened the portfolio, with all the other women watching, found that everything was soaked. Both copies of my speech were ruined, and my entire brand new note pad was useless. I heard one of the women laugh. It added to my overall unfamiliar insecurity. Panic set in for the next few minutes.

Then, I stopped and prayed.

I decided I would write down as much as I could remember and simply do the best I could. I still had an hour-and-a-half until my time slot, so I removed my pen from the portfolio and began asking for a sheet of paper.

My life changed in a deep way that day.

The first woman I asked, who had a portfolio like mine, but with a thicker notepad, said "no," adding she needed her paper. I remember being shocked that she'd said no. Of course she didn't owe me her paper, but it was shocking she wouldn't give me a sheet, especially given my circumstances. I moved on to the next woman. One after another, and with a variety of excuses, I was told that I couldn't have a sheet of paper. One woman had a smirk on her face, and I thought she had to have been the one who laughed, although I can't be sure. Everyone had paper except for two of the younger women, one who had her speech written on the folded up paper in her hands, the other had her speech on index cards. I resigned myself and had all but given up when the younger woman who had her speech on index cards, came up to me with a pamphlet from the conference. She said there was space at the end for conference attendees to take notes.

I wanted to cry. Not because of the insecurity and betrayal I felt at all the women who wouldn't help me; I wanted to cry because of the one woman that did.

Inspiration hit me suddenly, and I started writing. Everything just poured out into those few small pages in the back of that pamphlet.

As the conference commenced, I watched from the special section up front as a couple of the women got up, one after the other, to speak. Each of them talked about the power of determination and perseverance. How nothing should stand in your way as you power through and overcome every obstacle. They each gave a list of their accomplishments in life. I realized my original speech had been similar to all of theirs, not very original. When it was my time, I took a deep breath, walked across the stage, adjusted the microphone for my height, and started.

I showed the audience my pamphlet and the speech in the back. I told the same story I just told you: about being so excited to speak there, my husband helping me perfect my speech and buying me the brand new satchel. I told of the crowded room, the rain, and leaving my very special satchel behind. I laughed a bit as I talked about giggling in the rain, and then got serious as I addressed my sudden unfamiliar insecurity at the way my umbrella partner looked at me in disgust. When I got to the part about nearly tripping and watching as my portfolio catapulted into that puddle, I heard a gasp cycle through the crowd. I mentioned the loss I felt when I opened my portfolio and found that the few sheets of paper left on the pad and my speech were ruined; I mentioned the laugh I heard from one of the other women. The audience gasped again.

Then, I told the part about asking the women who were speaking at the conference that day for a sheet of paper. How all of them who had portfolios or notebooks full of paper had said "no." I told about the one whom had her speech on paper, folded and wished she could help but had nothing extra to give me. Then, I told about the young woman, about my same age then, who only had her index cards. How she brought me the pamphlet, because it had empty pages in the back that I could use. How, as I was writing vigorously, that same young woman also brought me a cup of water.

Then, I said that the most important thing I think as women we can offer *is ourselves*;[24] That, when we lift up a friend, we all rise to new heights together. I told them that my dad raised my sisters and me in that basic principle, and I never really knew what it meant, until the exact moment when the woman gave me a free pamphlet and simple cup of water.

I received a lengthy applause when I was done and several women in the audience stood. I felt accomplished. I felt I delivered the very message I needed to deliver that day, and I had no doubt someone needed to hear it.

After being seated, the next speaker was announced. She walked across the stage holding her notebook, evidently uncomfortable. A visible murmur broke out over the audience.

Her speech followed the same path as the others before me. She lined out how women must persevere. How we must make our way, no matter the sacrifice. She stumbled on her words a bit here and there, no doubt remembering my speech and her actions earlier.

Also, knowing that each audience member knew as well.

She continued, explaining how we had to work harder than men. Then, she laid out all of her many professional accomplishments for women throughout the years.

It was almost ridiculous to listen to after knowing she wouldn't give even one sheet of paper to another woman.

She received no applause as she exited the stage.

The next speaker, the young woman, index cards in-hand, walked across the stage to take her place at the microphone. She received a full house standing ovation. It didn't take long for me to realize it wasn't my message that mattered that day. It was that my message pointed everyone toward her message. Everyone listened intently as she talked about growing up with a mom who was drunk most of the time and a dad who worked a lot. He was a good provider, but left her to handle everything her mother neglected, including a younger sibling. I'm ashamed to admit, I don't remember if it was a brother or sister. When she was in middle school, her English teacher gave out an assignment to the class: write a paper about their home life. One day after school, the teacher asked her to stay behind, and the first thing the teacher told her, after all the other students were gone is, "You don't need a mother."

Of course the audience gasped, including me.

She continued to tell that the teacher explained that she needed to stop pitying herself and notice that God can, and will, put many women in her life that will help her. The teacher asked her if she had any unanswered questions that she would ask her mother if she could. She replied, "Yes."

The teacher responded, "Shoot."

She told the attentive crowd how that day marked a new beginning for her. She would always recognize the women in her path that helped her. When she first had to use the laundromat, because their machine broke, a woman showed her how to use the big machines and gave her detergent. When she first started learning to drive, a neighbor woman used her own car and took her every day after school, to learn. When it came time for college and she didn't know where to start, an admissions woman helped her fill out paperwork and secure her grants, scholarships, and loans. When she first started looking for a job and needed a résumé, a woman in the library helped her create one. When she got married, she gained a solid woman in her mother-in-law, who helps her all the time.

She learned through her young life that we all have women who help us. "Unfortunately," she paused, looked at me, and stated, "we also have women who don't. Sometimes, even women who will try and sabotage us."

She stated that she'd learned in her young years that often women who don't help were ones who didn't recognize when they were helped. They take sole credit for their achievements. Many may have grown up in their own self-pity, even used it to drive them to get ahead. While they do exist, very, very few women ever really make it all on their own.

She paused, the audience (including me) was so enraptured that you could've literally heard a pin drop. She then stated, "Somewhere along the way, we as women, must make a decision. It is unavoidable. We must decide which woman we want to be: the hunter or the helper."

She received a standing ovation as she

walked off the stage. After her, many women in the audience left, in mass at first, then a trickle throughout the day. No more than ten or fifteen remained when the keynote speaker walked across the stage to deliver her speech. It was awkward, and I did feel sad for her. Her notepad was still full, but I could see she regretted that it was. I'm pretty sure she became a helper that day.

That young girl's story impacted me so much that I started to recognize each woman who helped me along the way, and there have been many. Because that story about her teacher also impacted me so much, I included it in one of my novels. It was a turning point for me.

Unfortunately, back in the early nineties, we didn't have social media. The young woman from the conference and I didn't exchange information or keep in touch. I always regretted not getting more information about her, but I've learned since then that not all women are meant to stay in your life.

Some are there for a season or a reason.

Maybe, in something as quick as a trip to the convenience store, someone will impact you. Others will be in your life longer, like some of my lifelong friends. Some women won't want your help, because they aren't used to it. They may even doubt it, because what woman helps another woman for no reason, right? We've all run in to the helpers and the hunters. We've all played the adversary as well as the ally.

I am thankful today to have many beautiful and gracious women in my life, women who help and inspire me. I have enemies, but I have more encouragers, and for that I count myself fortunate. My hopes are that I do the same in return and always try to recognize those women who help me along the way.

Which woman are you?

The hunter or the helper?

The enemy or the encourager?

The adversary or the ally?

Sometimes, I think in life, *we all* have to make that choice again and again.

24. Romans 14:19

Be a Builder

Marcie Klock

Friendship is a beautiful and wonderful thing when shared authentically; when not, it's corrosive. The truth is, we should all have an arsenal of friends we can rely on, trust, who are authentic and honest with us.

We aren't meant to go through life without friends, but frankly friendship can be messy.

Recently, I was reflecting with my closest girlfriend about a period in my life where I had some friendships that did not bring out the best in me. Not only did those relationships not bring out the best in me, but I also was not at my best. My life was messy during this period, and I was traveling most of the time for my career. I was also raising a small boy as a single parent, and just trying my best to juggle both worlds. My travel would have me going to and from the East Coast in Virginia to the beautiful West Coast, California.

I realize with much hurt, anger, and sadness, that these friendships weren't really productive in my life. In the end, they eventually outgrew me, or I outgrew them. Yet without them, I wouldn't have grown enough to realize it.

Friendship like any relationship should not be based on dishonesty or deceit. Relationships are much like plants when you think about it; they need nourishment, water, light, sun, care, and food to not only grow, but stay alive.

I think we must always be evaluating the people in our lives and take a serious look at our inner circle. It may sound weird, but if you are a Christian, it's important that our friendships are, in fact, based on the right things. Our truths. Our authenticity.

It has taken me years to come to this conclusion.

Friendship, like any relationship, can be messy at times, especially for us women. We

231

are emotional human beings.

Whatever friendships we have now, it is vital they are formed to help sharpen us through any crisis we go through. More importantly, through that crisis, can you count on those in your circle for honesty? Can God work through them to relay something to you that you need to hear?

I have a girlfriend who literally sets me straight in a way that I know is a gift from God. This does not mean she is harsh to me. She speaks with grace and love, but most importantly, she doesn't hold back things just to satisfy me or make me happy. In addition, her words are never meant to degrade me or bring me down. They are meant to edify and encourage. That is real friendship. That is what our arsenal of close friends should be made up of. Those friends that can be honest with us, even in those moments where honesty may be hard for us to hear. We should go through life with friends that will go to battle with us.

My Spirit-driven, authentic friendships know that I talk openly about my own, deeply personal flaws. We are all flawed human beings, and I'd like to hope God uses me to help my friends, just like they help me.[25]

I believe women were meant to stick together,

to support one another. We need each other, mostly when we have or encounter problems. Unfortunately, not all women do support other women.

When I reflect back to being a young girl and think of the women in my family and how they stuck together and supported one another during difficult times, my heart always fills with love. They banded together.

I grew up in Church as a young girl and also played sports. I was exposed and witnessed a lot of women stick together throughout my life as a child and as an adult, but I've also seen the opposite. I've witnessed the women who tore one another down, who intentionally caused strife between other women. Women who gossiped[26] and spread secrets.[27]

One of my best girlfriends said to me once, "Marcie, you need to write. You have a voice for women, to encourage and build them up."

That was God. I'm not talking about my writing … I'm talking about this woman who built me up, instead of tearing me down.

25. Proverbs 27:17
26. Proverbs 16:28
27. Proverbs 11:13

Sister by the Blood

Kristi Williams Fontenot

If you have siblings, consider yourself lucky. I honestly cannot say that I never remember wanting a sibling as a child, but as an adult sometimes I face challenges that would make life easier if I had siblings. My parents didn't intend on having only one child, however God makes those plans. Nonetheless, not having siblings has opened my eyes to the blessing that brothers and sisters are to each other. As a mother myself, God has blessed me with four children, and I remind them often to never take each other for granted. There are times, as they have grown, that they haven't always been the best of friends, but there is no doubt, as they have gotten older, they are. And no matter what, they have always been there for each other when the going gets rough. Having siblings is indeed a blessing! It's like having a built-in friend for life.

Maybe you are like me, an only child, or maybe you're not. Thankfully, God has provided me with sisters in Christ that have come alongside me to be there for me as a sibling would normally do. I can count them on one hand, but each of these women have been there for me when I need them, regardless if I have talked to them this week or not for a month. They are here with me to praise God through life's victories as well as coming along side me to walk through the valleys in life the devil throws at me.

Just like when I was pregnant with my fourth child, we were told of many disabilities our son would have. My husband and I went to doctor's appointment after doctor's appointment only to hear our news was much of the same. I was walking through a very tough season in my life, and these women stood beside me in my time of need to pray over me. To be the listening ear that I needed. To help carry me when I felt I couldn't walk alone. And, ultimately, to praise God with me when we received the answers to all our prayers.

Thankfully, God never intended us to do life alone. And I don't mean that from a marriage standpoint. Many Christians will go through life without a spouse, but God does want us to surround ourselves with friends. Not just any friends, friends that pick each other up when one falls. Friends that are there to help carry our burden when it feels too heavy for us to carry alone. Friends to laugh with us, and to cry with us. You see, we all need people in our lives that will do life with us and be that good influence when we need it.

I like to think of this group of women as my tribe. The common denominator among us is our love for Christ, our love for our families, and our love for each other.[28] Thankfully, our sisters do not have to be blood for God to place them in our lives. They only need to be the people that will always be loyal to us no matter if we are walking on the mountain top or in the valley low.

It is also important to have those friends in our lives that will help keep us accountable. If our circle of influence isn't one that will lovingly correct us when we start to drift from God, then we need to find a new circle of influence. Even as Christians, we will all face times where the devil is trying to distract us from the path God has before us. We must surround ourselves with sisters-in-Christ that will come alongside us and point us back to Christ when we are drifting. Friends that will nudge us and say "Hey I've noticed that you haven't been in the group chat lately, is there something wrong?" Or "I've noticed you have been angry lately, is there something you would like to talk about?"

Life isn't always good, and there will be times that we may feel distant from God. That's when having sisters-in-Christ will be most important. We all need sisters that will not only love us and listen to us, but we need them to help sharpen us and guide us when we start to drift.

Friends are going to come and go throughout our lifetime. In my circle of friends, only one of these women has been a friend since I was a child. As you become closer to Christ, your circle of friends will begin to change. Maybe it will grow … or maybe God will remove people from your life that are not being helpful. The number of sisters doesn't matter and neither does the amount of time they have been in your tribe. They only need to have one thing in common … Christ. These sisters in my life love without judgement. They listen to what I say, but at the same time understand what I don't know how to say. These women make me a better person, and more importantly, they make me a better Christian.

Make sure your sisters do, too.[29]

28. Proverbs 17:17
29. Ecclesiastes 4:9-12

Friday the 13th

Colleen Crain

Friday the 13th is bad luck, people say, but for me, it's so much more. The pandemic basically turned the planet upside down. With orders to stay home and adopt a new way of life far from family, friends, and the familiar, it is a life-altering change. The "stay at home" and "social distancing" orders took effect in Louisiana on Friday, March 13, 2020, fifty years to the day since I faced my own death at an age one is not supposed to have the ability to understand what death is.

As I drove to an appointment the morning of the stay-at-home order, I was hit with the realization that I feel free. It makes no sense that after a lifetime—and I mean a lifetime—of life-limiting fear, hyper-vigilance, and anxiety that I would feel free in the midst of such uncertainty. Yet there I was, realizing I was finally free and willing to live and experience life with all its uncertainty.

Most of my life, I lived with an ever-present cloud of anxiety. Fear and anxiety that were intensified when my surroundings or my routine were out of my norm, or seemed unfamiliar. To feel safe, I needed to always know that my feet were on certain and familiar ground. I remember when it all started. It was the afternoon of Friday, March 13, 1970.

I can still see all the details of my bedroom – the closet, with two brand new little dresses hanging there. My mom had just finished making my new Easter dress and another ABC dress that little girls wore in 1970. I was so excited to get to wear them and put on my new shoes. Oh, I love shoes! My love of shoes must have started early, because I can see them all lined up in that closet.

I can see the little black-and-white TV on the metal rolling stand. That TV and my new favorite TV show are the reason I was alone in my room that afternoon. My brothers and sisters all preferred to watch *Gomer Pyle* on the big color TV in the den, but I loved the new show! I was simply happy to watch *Sesame Street*, even if I had to watch it on the little portable black-and-white. As I settled in, excited to see the man paint the number of the day, I remember smelling something strong and irritating. For some reason, I always associate that smell with burning tomato soup, but that's not exactly what it smelled like.

I sat on the edge of my bed, only now I was watching fire roll across the hall ceiling toward me. I really can't tell you why I didn't move or why I didn't scream. Maybe I froze out of terror. Though that day may have been my introduction to it, I know terror well. It followed me for over forty-five years. It followed me into elevators and forced me to walk the stairs—sometimes eight to ten flights or more, and often dressed in heels and other attire inappropriate for such a hike. It kept me out of car washes, amusement park attractions, and robbed me of experiences, situations, and likely lots of fun. It even kept me out of relationships in which there was a possibility I might be trapped.

I remember how loud it was in my room that

day. The roaring came with the fire as it reached my bed. I remember seeing people outside my window trying to break it with bricks or large rocks. I remember there came a point when my room filled with smoke and fire. I had to shrink back from it and climb onto my bed into the only space that was not yet burning. I could see my feet as I stood in the corner of my bed. They were small, but they filled that entire little space in which I stood. I remember later telling Momma that it was really like I was with the devil.

My room became dark—the darkest dark— no light at all. If there was anything in front of me, I couldn't see it. I tried to open my eyes wider, but the wider I opened my eyes, the darker it seemed.

Terror.

A couple of weeks before that Friday the 13th, I had become fascinated with the story of a little blind girl and how she managed to find her way in the world by reaching out and feeling along walls. In those weeks, I spent a great deal of my days practicing how I might make it in the world in case I ever lost my sight. I would close my eyes, reach out my arms, and feel my way around our house, my grandparents' house or wherever I happened to be. On more than one occasion, my mother firmly insisted I stop. I always thought that she thought I was making fun of blind people. I later learned that seeing me pretend to be blind caused a deeply disturbing feeling in her. As a mother, I now understand how upsetting it is to even imagine any difficulties our children may have to face.

On this day though, there was no thought of feeling my way along the walls. The walls were in flames, and my only thoughts were not really thoughts at all. There was no room for thoughts. I was fully occupied with those feelings of terror.

Outside, my uncles, grandparents, young brothers and sister were trying to find a way to get me out of the house. Each time my uncles tried the door nearest my bedroom, intensely burning flames came shooting out of the doorway keeping everyone away.

That door at the end of the hallway of the kids' rooms was a point of contention between my city-born and raised mother, and my country-boy father at the time that addition to the house was built. My New Orleans Momma believed too many entry points was dangerous, especially ones near children's rooms. My Northshore Daddy believed that a good number of exits were essential in case of fire. He grew up in the land of fire towers and far from any fire stations.

While the others were trying to find a way to get to me, my sister, Donna, nine years old at the time, approached the door again. She later told us that when she touched the doorknob, it was no longer hot and opened easily. The flames had calmed and were no longer shooting out of the doorway so she opened it wide and yelled as loud as she could for me to come out.

I didn't hear her though. I only heard the loud roar of the fire, and I still couldn't see anything. I couldn't see anything.

To this day, I don't know how I got out. I didn't move past the place just outside the doorway. I remember Donna pushing me away from the house. I wouldn't tell anyone that I couldn't see. I vividly remember everything else about that day, but I don't know how I got from that tiny spot on my bed to the space outside that doorway.

Within seconds of me clearing that doorway, the entire part of the house, completely engulfed in flames, collapsed in on my bedroom, followed by the rest of the house. The entire house was gone. Nothing was saved—except us, every one of us. My parents and oldest sister arrived home shortly after the house fell.

God rescued me from the flames, and I have no doubt whatsoever that He did.

I am as sure as I am of the skin covering my body that God rescued me. He wrapped me up and carried me out. I don't remember it, but I am completely convinced of it. In that house—that fully-engulfed house—God protected me and carried me. The only physical evidence to others that I was ever in that fire at all, were the little blisters on my feet.

Internally, I *knew* that I was dying. I knew I swallowed fire, because I could feel it, burning me from the inside out. I could feel it burning me up inside my chest. I knew that if I let go of the person holding me, it would be the end.

I still couldn't see, but there was no way I would tell anyone.

My eyes burned, and I couldn't hide that kind of pain from my mother. I remember when I arrived for medical treatment I lied to Momma, "they don't hurt anymore, Momma." It was the first time that typically-good, patient Colleen didn't want to see a doctor.

Terror.

People say you don't remember pain, but I remember thinking I hated whoever was putting those drops in my eyes every day. About a week after the fire, my eyes healed, and I regained my sight.

I know that on that Friday the 13th, and every day since, God rescued me—saved me. No matter what happens, I know God keeps me. He rescues me. He prepares me with practice to survive and thrive. He prepares me; and he prepares the places I will walk with blessings and escape routes.

Since that day, I've always known that God is ever-present. However, somewhere deep inside, even though I've always trusted Him to keep me and believed I was a miracle, the fear and dread was still there. Not the fear of death, the fear that I might be trapped one day and have to experience those feelings again.

After spending most of my life running from the ever-intensifying power this fear had over my life, with the encouragement of my daughter, I sought the help of a wonderful Licensed Professional Counselor. It took work, trust, and giving up the idea of a "cure" or a perfect journey. I learned to be patient and walk the walk that was in front of me. Feel it, experience it, and accept the struggle. I accepted that the struggle may from time-to-time still bother me, but I no longer needed to run from it. I learned to be comfortable feeling uncomfortable. I may even "fail" and "freak out" on an elevator or a

Disney ride ... oh yeah, I've done that. I can feel it and move on without shame or the belief that I was cursed to always be limited by this fear.

This life, the one now, feels different than I expected. It feels real. It feels grounded—not like the magical easy cure for which I prayed and always thought I wanted.

While praying one morning during the shut-in, these words came to mind, "The only real freedom is in Christ."

Then, I thought of Patrick Henry's famous quote, "Give me liberty or give me death."

I choose *freedom.*

I am free to live. God is in control no matter what happens. I am thankful beyond my ability to express it, for His grace, love, and protection. I thank Him for knowing me, creating me, understanding me, being patient with me, and delivering me—not just that day, but every day!

For me, every Friday the 13th is a day of remembrance and thanksgiving. It's a day I celebrate how God preserves me, protects me, and for which He prepares me and my surroundings.

Fear of Death

Megan Taunton

I held my newborn baby girl for the first time; she weighed a whopping six pounds. She was the baby I prayed for. The baby I thought may never happen. The light at the end of a tunnel. I never planned or imagined that just in five shorts years, I would have to hold her again like a newborn, lifeless, helpless, pale, and ravaged by cancer. I would have to release her to a coroner, and not the nursery nurse. At just three years old, my daughter was diagnosed with a terminal brain stem tumor that wrecked every part of her body, stealing her physical abilities, but leaving her mind to observe and understand.

I know that's tough to read, but it happens. It happens every single day. Kids die. They die before they have lived a long life where they graduate, get married, have babies, grow wrinkly and gray. They die at only five years old. I knew this, but it was one of those things you push away. You shove so hard, trying to push away the "what ifs" and "maybes," because just to imagine it, is heart-stopping. I had fear that gripped me horribly, but what my journey has taught me is that we need not live in fear, but understand it. We need to recognize the level of compassion, the love, that comes from imagining.

The night my daughter passed away I lay in her bed, holding her stuffed Lambie, "Doc McStuffins," that she took everywhere, and I prayed. I prayed, "God please don't let me turn bitter. Don't let me be overcome with anger and rage. God just make this better" A death I knew was inevitable. Bits and pieces of my precious daughter, I grieved one-by-one. But in the moments, as you watch the process of a slow death, parts of you that are healthy become heightened. You find a new perspective. God opened doors in my mind I never expected. He also spoke loudly in my head, comforting me as each new emotion rose up.

Months and even years now after her death, God continues to challenge me to question instincts associated with death. Everything that I was taught or observed growing up about death was put into question. As a Christian, we are taught not to fear death, yet I don't think I remember observing that. As a child, we are taught by our parents to drive safe, don't do this or that. With the big stuff like car wrecks and drugs, we were taught that they would lead to death. Churches would gather around sick ones to pray for healing on earth, crying out as they asked repeatedly for deliverance from an illness, an accident, or cancer. As a child, I saw that as being fearful of death.

To face death head on with one of my most precious gifts, I have learned that it is not death that we should fear, but the absence of a relationship with God. I lived most of my life fearing that I would miss out on events in my own life; events like marriage, kids, and growing old. Eternal life was something to dream about and accomplish when I was older and ready ... after I had accomplished all I needed to do.

Now it seems silly to me, to have wasted so

much of my young life fearing that I would die early and miss out on so much.

We spend so much of our lives planning our futures instead of living our lives, enjoying the moments, and looking for ways to uplift others. My perspective has transformed death into a victory. An amazing transition into what we should be hoping for. Heaven should be our plan. I now think that anything this earthly life could offer me does not compare to what my Heavenly Father has in store for me.

This life will throw stuff at you, gut punches and tragedies, but we have the opportunity to walk through it for whatever time we are given, with the gift of living without fear of death.

If we walk by faith, focusing on the now and not the fear of what the future may bring,[30] we can walk in confidence of His love and His plan to take such amazing care of us and use our fearlessness to witness.

I watched my beautiful daughter who loved Jesus, transition into her eternal life without any fear of what was to come...

In Memory of Aiden Hilie Taunton (January 25, 2012- June 4, 2017)

30. Matthew 6:34

Love is not a Sprint, it's a Marathon

Erin Vavasseur

The first time I had ever laid eyes on him in 2010, I just knew he was the one. Of course, what sixteen-year-old girl didn't believe in love at first sight? He was beautiful, had long, shiny brown hair, piercing green eyes, and a perfect smile that seemed to light up the world.

My world.

In August 2012, I had just graduated high school, gotten my braces off, began perfecting my makeup skills, and started my first semester at Southeastern University. Everything was going so well. I had logged onto my Facebook one day and noticed I had a new friend and message request from Austin. Not long after, we began texting every day. After a week of nonstop conversation, we finally agreed to meet. No words could describe how excited and nervous I was to meet this man. But those anxious feelings melted away like butter when we first locked eyes. He was so dreamy. His smile was more gorgeous and contagious in person. He was witty, intellectual, talented, and kind. I was in love with the way he looked at me. We began dating just a few days later. *This is it,* I thought to myself, *My fairytale ending! He is perfect. Everything is perfect!*

The first few weeks were amazing. We became inseparable, and I was in love. He began introducing me to all his friends. Not long after, I became a part of their group; I started seeing a difference in Austin. They were using Opiates. I had experimented with a few things here and there over the years, but never really got into pills. It made me uneasy at first, but then, I would look at him, still the beautiful, witty, and charming guy, and I thought it would be fine.

Only it wasn't fine, and before long, I began using also.

Days, weeks, and months flew by, but they were a blur. The days were the same. The walls were the same. Life was an endless cycle of the same routine of making phone calls, bank withdrawals, and sketchy meet-ups.

December was supposed to be a great month. We were going to have our first Christmas together and Austin's best friend was turning twenty-one. That day, we had all made the promise to stop using drugs. I felt that things were finally turning around. The birthday came, and we ended up getting a hotel room in New Orleans for one last "hurrah!" A night filled with friends, music, and lines on the table led to a morning car ride home full of promises to never touch that stuff again. We all went home and went our separate ways. Back to the real world, to normal. Only it wasn't normal. Austin became distant. We were no longer inseparable. Days would go by where I wouldn't hear from him at all.

I grew worried. *Had he found someone else? Did I do something to upset him?* When I was finally able to reach him, he mentioned he had been extremely ill, and was sorry for being distant. He even apologized for forgetting Valentine's Day and wanted to do something special for me. I was instantly reassured of our relationship. I couldn't wait to see him again. The next day, I arrived at his parent's house to discover the kitchen full of heart balloons, candy, steaks, and Austin down on one knee. I was over the moon and with teary eyes; I jumped into his arms and said "Yes!"

Nothing could've been better.

Weeks later, I was at his house while he was at work. I wanted to do something nice for my soon-to-be husband, so I decided to clean his room. I remember opening the closet and immediately my eyes were drawn to the floor. There was a black leather jacket stuffed under the bottom of a wooden chest. It looked intentional though, and something in me just couldn't let the thought go. As soon as I picked it up, I saw that under the chest, and behind where the jacket had been, was a smaller wooden box. I could feel my heart sink and the hairs on the back of my neck tingle. I don't really know why, other than maybe intuition, but I just knew it would contain something bad.

Inside the box were five syringes, some elastic, and a vial of Naloxone. Tears began to fall. I had no idea what Naloxone was, but the syringes were enough to figure it out.

He had never stopped.

I was flooded and overwhelmed with so

many emotions, but especially hurt, rage, and betrayal. Nothing I had ever experienced could have prepared me for something like that.

How could I be so oblivious and blind?

How could he do this to me?

I began picking through the memories, and only then did I see the signs. Him being distant and sick all of the time. Him wearing flannels in the hot Louisiana heat, possibly to hide the track marks. Part of me wanted to leave right then and there. Instead I demanded answers. The second he walked through the door, he could tell by the look on my face that I knew. He fell to the ground, sobbing, and explained everything. How he was struggling every day since New Orleans. How he went from snorting to shooting. How sick he became every time he tried to stop. How he couldn't stop. I no longer trusted, but I also couldn't ignore his cry for help. I put my hurt aside and told him that we would get him the help he needed. I told him I would stay by his side and everything would be okay.

Thirty days. I didn't get to see him for thirty days. I spent most of the time questioning him, myself, and our relationship. *How do I move past these feelings of anger and betrayal? Will I ever learn to trust him again?* My mind raced with thoughts of the unknown until his "graduation." I was ecstatic and relieved to see Austin walk out the doors of the rehabilitation center. There he stood: my happy, handsome, and healthy man. He was back, and we could finally work on our own road to relationship recovery.

Austin's time was quickly consumed with AA meetings, sponsors, and step work. He was sober and busy. That was great, but I couldn't help but feel a little upset, because I was no longer a priority. Months passed, and there had been no time for us to work on our relationship and the damage done to it. When I decided to bring this to his attention, I was shocked when he agreed. I was heartbroken and devastated. I took off running, no destination in mind, tears falling behind with every stride. This was the ending I never saw coming. After exhausting myself, I sat down on a curb and cried for what turned into hours. When there were no tears left, I called my mom to pick me up and left without saying goodbye.

I was in pain, so much pain. How could these emotions feel so physical? I, once again, felt betrayed. After everything I had done; loving and supporting him through his addiction and the recovery process, the end of our relationship was the thanks I got. Not more time or effort like I'd afforded him.

Nothing.

Over time, the hurt and betrayal turned into anger and then depression. Not long after that, I began to feel nothing at all. Not even the desire to stick around the area. Everywhere I looked, I was reminded of him, so I packed up everything I owned and drove twelve hundred miles to Fountain, Colorado.

Colorado was a beautiful breath of fresh air, a clean slate, and a new beginning. It was exactly what I'd needed. I started seeing someone and had gotten a restaurant job. The change of scenery, plus a new relationship, should have been enough to let go of my past with Austin and move on. It wasn't, though. There was not a day where I didn't think about him and wonder how he was doing. Every day, it began to eat at me more and more. On the outside, I was still smiling and seemingly happy, but inside was a war zone. I got to where I didn't want to eat, sleep, or even bathe myself. My body and mind were withering away to nothing. *I can't feel like this forever,* I thought. *I won't feel like this forever.*

On January 29, 2016, I was working the closing shift at the restaurant when my phone went off. It was a text from an unknown Louisiana number. All it said was: Erin? My mind went to one place, to one face: Austin's. It had been over a year since we had contact so it couldn't have been him, could it? It was, though. He reached out to let me know he had just completed a nine-month rehabilitation program in Florida and was moving back home with his new best friend. He also wanted to let me know that he was sorry for what he had done and how things had ended between us.

That was what I had been waiting for, an apology and some closure. I thanked him, and we exchanged a few more words and said goodnight. Only two days later, I received word from my Dad that his mom, my grandmother, had passed away. I bought a ticket on the first flight back to Louisiana.

Home.

Sitting in the empty airport at 8 a.m., I began to think of home. Everyone I loved, and everyone I had missed. Of course Austin was one of them, only his was on repeat. The more I thought about everything, I started to think of the whole thing as a sign from God, or the universe. Before I knew it, I had taken out my phone and started a new text. I had to know if Austin felt the same way. I let him know I was coming into town and wanted to get together to talk about everything. He agreed.

I guess I never realized how mentally and physically unwell I became while living up north. I weighed ninety-eight pounds when I made it back to Louisiana, almost unrecognizable. To be honest, even I didn't recognize myself most days. Being there, home, turned out to be the closest I'd gotten to feeling like me in a long time. It was then that I realized I never should have left. I couldn't really outrun my hurt anyway.

When it was time and I was ready to meet with Austin, I sat there waiting for his car to pull up. I felt those all-too-familiar feelings. I was nervous and excited, similar to the first time we ever met. Something was different though, because I also felt scared. The last year-and-a-half, I had been living inside of my mind. So many "what ifs." I'd almost forgotten what it felt like to feel alive and present. As I heard the sound of tires on the gravel, my anxiety slipped away.

There he was.

He was the most happy and healthy I had ever seen him. He seemed different, but in a good way. We sat outside all night and reminisced over our time together, and apart.

The very next day, I made the decision to move back home.

It did not take long for us to become inseparable again. I had fallen in love all over again, but now for different reasons. He had changed over our time apart. He was more compassionate and mindful, emotionally invested in everything he did. He became more passionate about music, and started writing with his new friend. I wondered if our timing just hadn't been right before, because then, everything really felt perfect. The three of us decided to move in together. And when I thought things couldn't get any better, we found out I was pregnant. I never felt more complete, and couldn't wait for the following months leading up to our new family.

I began noticing little things here and there; his friend and Austin not being home when they were supposed to, money missing, the seclusion and the tiredness. Something about it felt too familiar. I decided not to wait, and approached Austin about the situation. I told him I was concerned for him and our roomate's sobriety. He told me I was just overthinking things because of our past, but that I was worrying over nothing. I felt irrational for thinking that they might have slipped up. I wasn't being

261

irrational, though. Weeks later, our roomate almost overdosed in our apartment. I know this sounds calloused, but I was just thankful Austin wasn't using again. I had felt maybe he was, but he assured me he wasn't, and I wanted to believe him. Not long after that, Austin and I sat him down and told him that he had to move out. We could not risk putting our son's life in danger over his drug use. He was sorry, I could tell, but then he was gone, and I believed that was the end of that nightmare.

Maybe I was so stressed out from the pregnancy hormones. I had extreme morning sickness and preeclampsia, so my doctor put me on bedrest for the remainder of the pregnancy. Austin was working two jobs, so I almost never got to see him. But when I did, there were red flags. He was always falling asleep or sick. Any time I would ask if these things were related to drug use, he assured me they weren't. He'd said he was just so tired from working all of the time. Deep down I knew, but I wasn't ready to know. We were about to have a baby, and I simply couldn't face it. The whole thing was swept under the rug, until our son was three weeks old. I came home from running errands and noticed both Austin and Finn, our son, were gone. I called Austin a few times. It rang and rang, but he never picked up. I began to panic and blow up his phone.

Finally, after many times, he picked up. He said he was at the gas station one mile away from our house and would be back any minute. Thirty long minutes later, he pulled up at home and went straight to the bathroom. I was sitting on the couch rocking Finn, when I heard an alarm go off from our bathroom. I knew something was wrong. I handed Finn to our new roommate and went to see what was going on. The bathroom was locked, and the timer was still going off. Something was really wrong. I started to scream and banged at the door, kicking until it opened. My heart stopped when I saw Austin. He was passed out on the toilet, blood dripping down his arms, with a syringe lying on the floor. I put two and two together and realized the timer was to wake him up. I remember screaming and yelling, shaking him to come out of it. Thankfully, he did quickly. I learned after that he had set a timer for himself just in case he nodded off.

How could he do this again?

Now, not only to me, but also our beautiful baby boy. I called his mother, and we found another rehabilitation facility. The familiar feelings returned. All the hurt, anger, depression, betrayal, and resentment. I wondered if our life would always be this vicious cycle.

I knew something had to change.

Austin stayed at that facility for thirty days. The facility itself was absolutely disgusting, but he said he had gained the most knowledge of sobriety and recovery from that place. I thought to myself, *if he could change his perspective, maybe I could as well.* I tried to stop seeing his repeated acts as purposeful and malicious, and instead, tried to focus on seeing the overall addiction that it really is.

When he got out, he started AA again. As soon as he felt he had things under control, he stopped attending the meetings, and stopped putting the work in. He got too comfortable. Not long after that, he slipped into the addiction again. Sometimes, the hurt and anger would surface. Other times, compassion and understanding.

In 2019, our former roommate, overdosed and died. As a result, Austin started a long bout with heroin. I imagine he, like I, had feelings of guilt. Only we had to deal with those things in ourselves. He felt he had to use as a coping mechanism. It is unfathomable to understand why, when a friend dies from a drug overdose, that anyone would dare even think of using, let alone do it.

But addiction doesn't work rationally.

I came to a fork in the road. I had a decision to make. Was I going to be there for Austin as a friend, a support? Or was I going to abandon him?

I had been shamed by others in the past for staying with him, but I've come to realize addiction isn't a sprint, it's a marathon.

So is love.

It's a marathon we will be running together. I've heard of tough love, and I get where people are coming from, but leaving an addict alone to die isn't love. I get boundaries; we have them in our marriage. I also get accountability, we have that, too, because we have a child who deserves a safe environment. But I also get free will ... and ultimately I can only use my own.

Austin has been completely drug-free for a year now. He is working hard and trying to be his best. He understands he can't do it alone, and he still goes to meetings. He's being the best father to Finn, and he helps other addicts who need help. He made a choice not to abandon them, too.

I've changed. I am no longer angry, nor do I feel the pain or resentment. Through everything I find I have strength, patience, and a resilience I didn't know I could have. I'm not going to lie and say it's easy, because truth is, problems aren't. I have learned that being a helpmate, a soulmate in life, isn't a cure-all for every problem. The happily ever after is in knowing we found someone who will be there, be support for each other, to help us make it through, and vice versa.

I've learned it's okay to leave ... but it's okay to stay also.

I'm not going to lie and say I pray, talk to God or a higher power every day in hopes it'll be a cure-all, because I don't. But I do believe in grace more than I ever have. With Austin's latest slip-up, I feel that God must feel the same about all of us, because we all slip-up.

I simply told Austin, "I'm just so glad you are still here with us."

Defining Life

Karen K. Scott

Life has a way of molding us into the person we're meant to be. Every problem that occurs in your life is simply a test or a lesson. The tricky thing about life is you have only until your time expires to get it right, and your life has no "best before" date.

I was in a mentoring session one day, and there was a group of young people who were either living in foster care or being raised by their grandparents. None of these kids had the ideal living situation. We're talking about at risk, impoverished youth. They were given a fill-in-the-blank poem called the *I Am Poem*. It was so encouraging to see what each one thought of themselves. One young man wrote, "I am loving and special. I wonder if I'll be a father one day. I hear children laughing. I see a house in a nice neighborhood. I want to help people in need. I am loving and special." Those children have been dealing with problems out of their control, some homeless at times, and yet most of them still found a way to hope for a brighter future.

How many times has life dealt you a bad hand, a bad day, and you've decided to handle it negatively? Each situation you face is molding you into the person you're meant to be. The crazy thing is, until you pass the test, you'll keep repeating the lesson.

Problems will happen. You may feel like a failure at times. However, the only true failure is in giving up. You have to keep at it and hold yourself accountable for you and no one else. The young man who was reading his poem later shared that he refused to be a result of his parents' bad decisions. He would be a product of his decision to live his life to the best of his ability.

Talk about encouraging.

Speaking things into existence. Speaking

positive things into your life. Having a positive attitude. These are all tools used to overcome your negative situation.

This young man decided to conqueror his problems. He knows that his attitude towards life is a direct reflection of his outcome. For the Bible says God will bless you if you don't give up when your faith is being tested.[31]

Never let your problems define you, let them mold you into being a better human, wife, husband, mother, father, brother, sister, or friend.

The key to conquering your problems is to share them, remember you're never alone. Oftentimes we let pride or fear keep us in solitude. Reach out to someone, and ask for help. There is a freeing spirit in asking for help. Not only are you being vulnerable, you're allowing someone else to bless you, help you in your need. This could be as simple as a word of encouragement, reassurance, direction, or a testimony. You could be a blessing by letting someone bless you.

Then, you persevere by taking the next step.

31. James 1:12

But God

Kristi Williams Fontenot

It was late 2007 when my husband and I found out we were expecting our fourth child. As we sat together for our Valentine's Day date night, baby names were the topic of our conversation. I loved the name Elijah and my husband loved the name Eli. One thing Brady and I have always agreed on was our children's names. We never discussed another name, and I still find it funny that I can remember these little details. God always knows what He is doing in helping us remember all the little details to the story, ultimately testimony which He creates.

Exactly one week later we were heading to the hospital to find out the gender of our newest bundle of joy. I still remember it like it was yesterday. I had to go to work after our appointment, and Brady was coming from work, so we met at the hospital. Like every time before, we went into the ultrasound room with anticipated excitement to see our baby for the first time on the monitor. After the sonographer finished taking measurements of the baby, she quickly started showing us our baby's fingers and toes. It is always amazing seeing your baby for the first time. Before the ultrasound was over, she showed us what we both knew all along: *It's a boy!* The sonographer left the room and Brady kissed me as he walked out the door heading back to work.

What happened next would change my life forever.

As the tech returned to the room, she asked me to follow her to the doctor's exam room. I assumed I would be examined by the doctor, and that would be it. When the doctor came into the room, he asked me where my husband had gone. I told him he needed to get back to work and that he had left. He then told me that I needed to call him to come back to the

271

hospital, because he needed to talk to us about something.

In that moment, I knew we were about to hear something that no one wants to hear. I still remember sitting in that room by myself, thinking every bad thought that could possibly go through my mind. Once Brady arrived, the doctor began to tell us that the ultrasound had found a spot on our baby's liver that was a concern. He went on to tell us that babies born with these types of spots are usually born with several different complications. Deafness, blindness, and intellectual disabilities were a few of the things he went over with us. He told us that we needed to see the specialist, and that his nurse would make us an appointment as soon as possible.

Five days later, we were on our way to see the doctor at maternal fetal medicine.

A maternal fetal medicine doctor is a high-risk pregnancy doctor. We didn't really know what to expect for our appointment. When we were called back, the nurse proceeded to do a new ultrasound to show the doctor the area of concern. Once she was done, she asked us to follow her into the doctor's office. I remember sitting in his office looking out the window, crying, telling Brady nothing good would come from this meeting. We waited about twenty minutes ... it felt like an eternity. Once the doctor came in and introduced himself, he began to tell us the same news my doctor had told us just five days earlier. At that moment, I felt numb. I have never felt such emptiness, before or since, as I did in that doctor's office. All I could think about was how our life was changing so quickly, and knowing that I had absolutely no control.

Little did I know, God was in control.

Brady always assured me everything would be alright. As much as I loved him comforting me, the pain a mother feels is something a husband cannot comprehend.

Carrying a baby ... feeling that baby inside of you.

There is an instant connection mothers have with their unborn baby. The pain was devastating to me. I left the doctor and headed towards work. At the time, I worked for my dad in our small restaurant. I remember walking in the back door and completely losing it. I was devastated telling my mom and dad that our diagnosis hadn't changed, and we would be facing a number of different complications with our unborn baby. I still remember my dad telling me over and over again, "We will get through this."

When I got home ,the house was quiet, because the other kids were not home from school just yet. I walked to my bedroom and hit my knees in prayer. I sat on my knees in my bedroom with my Bible in my lap as I literally cried out to God. As I sat there crying and praying, I asked God to show me what He wanted me to know, to tell me what He wanted me to hear. Before this moment, I do not remember ever using my Bible as a reference for any troubles in my life, but in that moment, I referenced healing in my Bible. It brought me to eight groups of scripture. Out of all the scriptures, I read only two, but what I would read would be the beginning of a new relationship with God that I had never known or understood before.

The first scripture I read was in 1 Kings[32] and the second scripture I read was in James.[33]

After reading just those few pieces of scripture from God's word, my heart began to change from sadness to peace.

What were the chances that the only name my husband and I would discuss would be the same name God would give me in these two pieces of scripture?

What would be the chance that out of the

eight pieces of scripture, I would pick the two that would answer my question of what God wanted me to hear so clearly?

I knew in that moment it wasn't chance; it was God! God's word was showing me how, because Elijah had such a close relationship with God, that he truly believed that what he would ask of Him, God would give him! He had so much faith in God that he knew that jar of flour would not run out, nor the jug of oil, and the widow would have more than enough to feed everyone in her home. He had so much faith in God that he knew the God of the universe would bring the widow's son back to life if Elijah just cried out to Him in complete faith. He had so much faith in God that he knew if he prayed with purpose, and with intention, that God would answer his prayer for no rain and again answer his prayer for rain three-and-a-half years later. He knew that faith in *the* God above all things, was all he needed!

In that moment, my faith began to grow stronger. It was as if all of a sudden, my eyes were opened. Even after spending my whole life in church, I had never truly seen God or understood Him until that moment. There was a flood of peace that came over me that I had never felt before. An understanding that, even though I had absolutely no control, the God of the universe was in complete control. For the next five months, I went to appointment after appointment to see no change in my unborn baby's diagnosis, but all I could say to anyone and everyone that asked me how things were going, was that I knew my God was going to heal him. I not only prayed asking God to heal him, but I *thanked* God for healing him. The thing about faith is that it is unseeable, it is invisible. We cannot see God, yet we believe that He exists, that He listens to and that He answers our prayers.

The day Elijah James was born was a day that the unseeable faith became visable. The day Elijah James was born was the day God showed not only me, but also everyone in that delivery room, that our God is a God that listens to and answers our prayers. And above all else, the day Elijah James was born, was the day God showed us that He is a God of miracles. For months after Elijah was born I brought him to appointment after appointment only to be told that even though the spot is still there, he is completely healthy. At one time, they even thought he had cancer in his liver, because his bloodwork came back showing levels of concern. But when we went to see the doctors at

St. Jude, they re-ran all of his bloodwork, and his levels were all back to normal. All I could tell people was, but God. At the publishing of this book, Elijah James is twelve years old, and God has given him a story to tell.

A story of prayer, a story of faith, and a story of healing.[34]

Many people told us, after Elijah was born, that those doctors were wrong, but just what if those doctors were right? God has the final say in how the story ends either way. When I look at my blue-eyed miracle, I am reminded time and time again, that He alone is in control.

But God!

32. 1 Kings 17:7-24
33. James 5:13-18
34. Genesis 50:20

Then One Day, It Happened

Shannon Ory Smith

Our day-to-day lives tend to become monotonous, the same old thing, day-in and day-out. Perhaps because of my monotonous and seemingly-boring life, I have had a habit of consuming myself with other people's stories. Whether it was good or bad, happy or sad, if it intrigued my interests, I was sucked into the abyss and wanted to know more about the people in those stories. I often call myself the Google Queen, because I have this tendency to research and investigate anything and everything about things and people that spark my interest. Unfortunately, in some of those stories that I dive into, bad things have happened to good people.

Throughout my life, I, just like everyone else, have faced challenges, events, and obstacles that would take the wind out of my sails for a short period of time. Nothing significant enough to pull me down and defeat me long-term. Even though I had never faced anything that totally broke me, I still found myself restless with fear about what lurked around the next corner. My mother always told me I worried too much and needed to relax, but I could never do it.

Then, circumstances and real-life events that I thought would never happen to me and my family, became my reality and nightmare.

I was in Baton Rouge when my husband called. "Bronson's been in a bad accident, and I am on the way to the hospital!"

He had little information, so after we hung up, I immediately called the emergency room of the hospital in our town. They could only say that there was an accident victim en route to the hospital, and that the air ambulance helicopter was outside waiting for the accident victim to be transported due to the severity of the trauma.

I hung up and called my husband back to say the helicopter was waiting at the hospital, he then said, "I know. I am here, and it is not good."

I asked if he could see our son.

"I am standing right here by him," he replied, "They are loading him in the helicopter, they are pumping air into his lungs, because he is not breathing on his own. He is not moving, and his head is completely busted open, and there is blood all over him,"

I then asked where are they taking him, and I could hear the paramedics say Jackson, Mississippi, I said "Jake, please, please, please ask them to bring him here to Baton Rouge, so I can get to him quicker."

I was desperate to be with my son!

My husband asked, but they insisted they had to take him to UMMC (the University of Mississippi Medical Center) in Jackson, Mississippi, because of their excellent neurological trauma team, and they were more equipped to handle the head trauma. I asked how long it would take to get him there. They told my husband about thirty-five to forty minutes. My husband's dad and step mom had arrived at the hospital before the helicopter departed, so they were there and able to drive with my husband to Jackson, which is about one-and-a-half hours from our house and about three-and-a-half hours from where I was in Baton Rouge.

The last words my husband said was, "It does not look good, Shannon. *I don't think he's gonna make it.*"

Mom and I made unbearably long drive to the hospital. When we arrived, my husband met me outside the Trauma emergency room.

The despair is indescribable, but all I wanted to do was get to Bronson as fast as I could. Security would only let one back at a time, so I had to go in alone. The curtains were closed, and when I pulled them back, I saw my son, lifeless, with tubes and IVs, on a ventilator, still covered in blood. His face was so swollen, and there was no movement. I immediately started talking to him, so if by any chance he could hear me, I wanted him to know he was not alone, and *Momma* was there. I told him to fight harder than he has ever fought for anything.

Seeing him like that, even though I did not know what the future was going to hold for him, I knew my heart was telling my mind that he was not leaving this world. He was going to make it. I did not know to what capacity he would come back to us, but burying him was simply not an option in my mind.

I prayed harder than ever and talked to God constantly. I knew I had to totally surrender myself to God, because He was the ultimate source.

I hadn't realized that an army of prayer warriors was coming together, and word of Bronson's accident was spreading faster than I could have ever imagined.

Across Mississippi.

Across Louisiana.

State-by-state.

I had no idea that so many people could come together so quickly. I started receiving text messages and Facebook posts, also videos from friends of Bronson that I did not know, of him being the clown and jokester that he is. He always loved making people laugh and being the center of attention. One of those videos was of him singing the beginning part of Queen's "Bohemian Rhapsody" with the line "nothing really matters," and I treasured it.

They transferred Bronson to the Neuro Intensive Care Unit for more tests. A hole had been drilled in his skull and a catheter with a monitoring sensor was placed inside his brain to drain any fluid and monitor the pressure and swelling. Even though he was in a coma, and with the severity of his injuries, his vitals seem to maintain in ranges that no additional procedures needed to be done.

Throughout the next day he had several CT scans, an MRI, and an EEG. The following morning, the neurosurgeon came in with his team, and for the second time in days, I hear the words, "he is probably never going to wake up, and if he does, he will more than likely be in a vegetative state." To add, there was no surgery, medicine, or any type of procedure that could be done, and we were given the prognosis: Diffused Anoxal Injury (DAI for short), Grade III. I remember the tears flowing uncontrollably down my face. I found myself in the waiting area doing some research on my phone to find out exactly what DAI meant. What I found was that more than 90 percent of DAI, Level III brain trauma patients never regain consciousness, and 7 percent of them remain in a vegetative state. So basically, according to the scientific world, my son had a 3 percent chance of waking up and having some type of quality of life.

I cried out to God daily.

As time went on, even though all vitals remained good, his brain pressure stayed within normal range. There was no significant hemorrhaging, no additional swelling, we found out that the lower left part of his lung had collapsed, and he had pneumonia. However, soon his lung had begun to repair itself and was getting stronger. The abdominal bleeding that we were told of in the beginning had pretty much healed on its own.

Doctors started noticing him taking some breaths on his own, and day-by-day they were backing down on the ventilator and because he was responding to stimulation and touch, they were backing off sedatives.

Then on day ten, post-accident, the crew of neuro doctors came in for their morning assessment and made a decision to shut off sedation to see what would happen ... and within a few minutes, we noticed his eyes started opening. As time went on, his eyes opened more and more. Within thirty minutes, his eyes were completely open.

Our son was awake.

We watched him become more awake throughout the day, but we knew he was not aware of what was going on. It was like we were looking into his eyes, but they were so dark and empty; they kept rolling into the back of his head. We continued to talk to him and touch his hands. We both knew he was aware of us being there with him, because he was able to respond to us by squeezing our hands, or would blink.

Day eleven, post-accident, Jake and I brought headphones for him to listen to music, we both knew if anything could get him to come around, it was music. For certain reasons we started playing Queen's "Bohemian Rhapsody" and Bronson spoke his first words, "Nothing really matters." It was his normal voice, but almost like an infant. He knew the lyrics!

As each day passed, he continued with the progress and was seriously blowing the minds of the doctors, nurses, and medical staff. None of us could believe the hurdles he was overcoming and how quickly it was happening, but we all knew one thing for certain. It was all the work of God, and no one could deny it or take credit for it.

A few days passed, and we were told that he would probably have to have a tracheostomy, because once they took him off of all mechanical ventilation, he would need help to pump air into his lungs. However, within days, Bronson had overcome that obstacle and was totally breathing on his own.

After fourteen grueling, long days, on June 24, 2019, he was moved from Neuro ICU to the

Neuro Care Unit. Even though we had battles to bear, and there was a lot of frustrating times, he was pushing forward and was getting better with each passing day. After about three or four additional days out of the ICU, Jake stepped into the restroom and I was standing, rubbing lotion on Bronson's feet. He, all of a sudden, said, "Jesus is prophet, and everyone must repent to make it to Heaven."

I was stunned at what he was saying and I asked, "What did you say?"

He repeated it again.

I called out to my husband, and Jake came out of the restroom. I said, "Bronson can you tell Daddy what you just said?"

Again, for the third time, Bronson repeated, "Jesus is prophet, and everyone must repent to make it to heaven."

Know, that yes, we raised Bronson in church. He had been saved and gave himself to Jesus, but like a lot of teenagers, he had veered off the path for a while. But we were witnessing God perform healing on our son, and the words that Bronson was saying was not something that was an everyday conversation.

And just days before, he was in a coma and had a grim prognosis.

My husband was literally raised in church

and knew way more of the Bible than I did, so Jake sat on the edge of Bronson's bed and started talking to him, asking him questions. Bronson then told us things that could not be explained, and Bronson described what he saw and how beautiful it was. He told Jake that he "saw Jesus" and said, "He was beautiful and magnificent." Also, that he "felt so safe and warm" and knew he "was in a wonderful safe place."

An additional one-and-a-half weeks later, we were still facing many nights and days ahead, with no sleep for either of us. Bronson was coming off of so many strong pain medications, Fentanyl, Morphine and Demerol. Having to get him eating, and with enough nutrition to avoid having a feeding tube inserted, he was having what was called "storming." The best way I can describe storming is when the traumatic brain injury patient has no control over their body, meaning they flail their arms and legs, and flip flop uncontrollably. Their brain is trying to heal and rewire itself, but is basically going haywire because of the trauma. He would scream out loudly saying things that made no sense. Sometimes, he would say very ugly and hurtful things. I was watching my twenty-year-old son, all one-hundred-and-ninety pounds of him, having to start completely over. An infant in a man's body. He could not sit up on his own, he could not feed himself, could not hold a cup, could not brush his teeth or hair, had to wear a very large diaper because had no control over his urine or bowels. Of course, he definitely couldn't walk, but the one thing he could do was still read and still had his memory.

So many obstacles were being overcome; progression was being made, and everyday was another step in the right direction. We knew, without a doubt, that all of it was the work of God.

I wish I could say that this was all easy, but someone suffering with a traumatic brain injury is unaware of everything going on around them, and it's tough.

Thirty days, post-accident, July 10, 2019, and Bronson had defied all odds against him.

The first seven-to-ten days in rehabilitation were extremely difficult. He was still having some pretty rough storming episodes, however, he was also getting stronger by the day.

He hated rehab. Stuff that we easily take for granted like feeding yourself, tying your shoes, brushing your teeth, putting on your clothes, sitting up in bed, or even how to turn from one side to the other while in the bed, was hard for him. And of course, he had to learn how to walk again. By the time our stay in rehab was coming to an end, he had been required to relearn so many things, just about everything really.

Thirty days in rehab, a total of sixty days post-accident, Bronson was ready to go home. We were sent home with a wheelchair and lists of orders we should follow, appointment schedules for follow-up visits with all his different doctors, and orders for out-patient rehabilitation.

Leaving the hospital was such a relief in itself, but it also opened up a whole new area of uncharted waters. I had been so focused on Bronson, that I hadn't taken care of myself. My mind, body, and heart started going into a downward spiral.

I started, what I now know, is a grieving process. It all hit me really hard, and I was dealing with a pain I had never endured before. I had guilt that I wasn't there and all the things I could have done differently to prevent this from happening to him. I became angry that his life was forever changed and that he had just turned twenty years old. I toiled over what kind of future he would have. On the outside, I tried my best to keep it together, to have a tough exterior, to be strong for my son, husband, and my family. On the inside, the pain consumed me, and I was tumbling out of control emotionally.

Soon after, most of Bronson's friends started to fade into the past and visits from family and friends became less and less. At this point, I started noticing the absence of people in my personal life. My lunch breaks at work were being spent in my car, parked in some random parking lot, crying for an hour, then pulling myself together to finish the day out. Then making the forty-five-minute drive home to prepare supper for my husband and son. My daily routine was literally tearing me down, piece-by-piece.

Bronson was handling it all way better than I was. I knew then that my son would be alright. He'd fight. And he'd overcome.

What about me? I had not overcome. Since the moment I received the call, and after putting together the events and circumstances surrounding his accident, I could not help but question why? Why was my son still alive and doing so well with such a positive progression in recovery? Why had it happened at all? The answer is, I don't know the answers. What I do know is within all of that is the plan of God.

I'm learning to trust that He knows where He is taking us, and I can honestly say I never lost faith in that fact. Do not get me wrong, I have questioned so much along the way, been confused, angry, hopeless, and even have had bouts of rage. I still deal with so many raw emotions regarding his injury. The Bronson I knew on June 9, 2019 is no longer here, and accepting that is a process also. But I have been given the most precious, priceless gift from God, and to me, in some ways, Bronson is better than he was prior to the accident.

I watch his positive attitude and his new appreciation for life, and it amazes me daily. I have no doubts that he will live a full life.

I am still personally striving to let God have all the hurt, confusion, and pain, but I have also learned that while life is short and unpredictable, God remains the way, the truth, and the light. I have seen his healing, and I am going to cling to it through my own struggles. I am no longer going to worry over tomorrow, because I have learned that today truly does have enough worry of its own.[35]

My monotonous and seemingly boring life is no more. I no longer have the habit of consuming myself with other people's stories. I have my own. And I am simply walking it out to find my purpose for God in it.

It is so true that, unfortunately, bad things happen to good people, but in sharing my story from fear, tragedy, despair, to trust, fortune, and hope, I will be able to help others cling to the truth that God remains in control. When I give up my will, for His, I can walk through the worst fears knowing a peace that truly passes all understanding and confusion.[36]

35. Matthew 6:34
36. Philippians 4:7

Surprised by God

Jacqueline Meier

In Genesis[37] Sarah was afraid, so she lied and said, "I did not laugh." But the Lord said, "Yes, you did laugh."

In the Old Testament, God promised Sarah and Abraham that they would have a son. They waited and waited on the promise. It seemed that it was a cruel joke that was never going to happen for them. Sarah got older and older and her biological clock appeared to stop ticking. Earlier in Genesis, a messenger tells Abraham that Sarah will give him a son. Sarah overhears the conversation and laughs.

Who wouldn't?

She was way beyond childbearing age at this point. It would be difficult for any woman to believe that it could still happen. The promise must have been a misunderstanding. How could she have a son? But, she did. God was true to His promise, even though it seemed impossible.

It happens.

That moment that someone comes up and asks you a personal question, that is really none of their business. The answer is something you might share with a really close friend without them needing to ask. But, there you are. You are probably facing a well-meaning person who is just trying to make conversation. How do you respond? I have been there many times. Several years ago, while struggling with infertility, a well-meaning person might ask "When are you going to start a family?" This usually happened at church. Discomfort... eyes averted... I found myself looking for an escape. A friend once told me that I should respond with "I don't know, what do you weigh?" That is not really my style though. Usually, I would quickly change the subject and excuse myself to the bathroom to hide in a stall and cry a little.

Those were hard years. I wanted children. I was already raising my young nephew. I had already spent years trying to get pregnant. I had seen fertility specialists and had gone through procedures and hormone treatments to no avail. The doctors had no answers for me. After all, I had gotten pregnant once several years earlier and had a miscarriage. I was heartbroken over that and mentally marked the date of the miscarriage every year for years. October 18th. It was always a sad day for me. What should have been, was not to be. My best friend was pregnant at the same time I was. She delivered her beautiful baby girl around the same time I was supposed to deliver my child. It surprised me that her baby girl stole my heart. I was afraid that I would resent her. Michaela was sweet and funny and a very special little girl.

A friend who was also trying to get pregnant ended up adopting a baby boy from Korea. I went over to her house to see him one week after she brought him home, and I fell in love. What a beautiful baby. I could do that. I could adopt a baby from Korea. It was set in motion so quickly. Agencies ... interviews ... paperwork ... lots and lots of paperwork.

Then, the call came.

I could hardly contain myself. "We have a

little boy for you, if you want him." I cried when I saw the pictures of this precious little boy. He was beautiful. He also came with a large number of medical concerns. I had to ask myself if I was up to the task of spending years of taking this child back-and-forth to medical facilities for surgeries and treatments with uncertain outcomes. I prayed ... and prayed ... and God spoke to me. Not in an audible voice, but still loud and clear. He reminded me of all the years that I had been pleading with Him for a child. He reminded me that there are no guarantees in life. Period. No guarantee I would ever get pregnant. No guarantee if I did get pregnant, that it would result in the birth of a healthy child. No guarantee if I was able to produce a healthy child, that it would remain healthy.

No guarantees.

He gently spoke to my heart, saying that He was offering me the opportunity to raise a son who needed me. How could I refuse God's generous offer?

So, I said yes.

A few months later, on September 30, 1989, standing in the Detroit airport, I held my son Zac for the first time. It was love at first sight. My life has never been the same. Then, came the doctor visits. A kind doctor at Mott Children's

Hospital at the University of Michigan Hospital assured me that he had treated hundreds of children like Zac. He said there is "no reason to think that your son will not have a normal life." Relief. Surgeries. Treatments. A little boy crying every time we drove into the hospital parking lot.

That was thirty-two years ago. He is thirty-three now. He is living a life of dreams and promise. He is married to a wonderful young lady who was adopted from China as an infant. God is good. And remarkably, October 18th came and went that year without notice. Not that I will ever forget the child I lost through a miscarriage, but my heart was full, and the memory of that loss was lessened.

Shortly after adopting Zac, I took him to visit my best friend and her sweet little girl, Michaela. I laid Zac down on a blanket and Mikki, who was four or five at the time, slowly circled him. She looked him over from every angle she could. She looked up, and in her sweet little voice she said, "Aunt Jackie, my grandma has a cat with a flat face." I told her that was interesting and asked her what made her think of that. She pointed at my dear, sleeping son's face. I laughed and said, "Mikki, do you think Zac's face is flat?" She smiled and nodded. To this day, she and Zac are close friends, but he won't let her forget that story.

When I think back about the time I was hiding in a bathroom stall, frightened that I would never know the joys of having children, it still makes my throat tighten up. However, if I hadn't gone through the longing for a child, would I have adopted Zac at all?

Likely not.

By the way, a month after I adopted Zac, I found out I was pregnant with my son Chris. He is thirty-one now, and God has blessed him immensely. Years later, after a divorce and remarriage, I gained two step-sons. So, in the end I played a part in raising five boys.

Be careful what you pray for. It seems that our God has a sense of humor. None of my children were accidents; they were planned by God, given to me in His way and with His timing.

37. Genesis 18:15

the Product of Focus

Marcie Klock

On December 28, 2019, I dusted off my journal and decided it was time to start writing again. Writing for me is therapy, and I find it very fulfilling.

Though, it had been a while...

Still, I had an overwhelming feeling that the theme was going to be very similar to something I had last journaled about. The word conflict filled me up, and not in the fruitful-goodness kind of way. I mean, conflict doesn't exactly fill us up with love, or give us warm, fuzzy, great feelings. I seriously don't know anyone who is desperately seeking or chasing conflict, although I know a lot of people who have it.

I know I personally prefer to sprint away from conflict as fast as my feet will allow me to. One of the best compliments I have been given throughout my life is that I have a joyful heart.

As I continue to grow my relationship with the Lord, while growing my faith, I am seeking desperately to be better than I was the day before. It is a choice and not easy to follow day-in and day-out.

Do you ever just pause to ask yourself why you are feeling a certain way? Are you actively seeking joy? Do you actively promote it by the way you live?

Sometimes, we have roadblocks that are joy-stoppers. If we are constantly chasing work, other people, or things, it becomes more and more difficult to find deep joy. Others aren't responsible for our joy; we are.

When I think of the word joy, a definition comes to mind and that is gladness not based on circumstances. So, when you really stop and think about it, it all comes down to our focus!

What am I focused on?

Am I focused on work and the fact that maybe things are not going as I planned? If so, my cup of joy is not going to be filled up. If we focused on our spouse to make us happy, and they are having an off day, then we are doomed to be joy-less! Especially, since then there would be two of us who need filling.

We are all responsible for our own joy, and *we don't get to place our lack of joy on another person.* We are responsible for creating and making a way to finding our own joy.

I have to keep in mind that some days, joy is a gift, and on other days, it is a battle. But when I take the time to focus on my thoughts, I really have the option to make a great day, greater, or a bad day, worse.

On January 6, 2020, a few days had passed since I had first dusted off the journal. Some major holidays also happened inbetween. That particular Monday morning, I woke up unlike I had for any other day in the previous six years. I was to be driving my husband to the airport that day, as he was flying back to his part-time home in Los Angeles, where he was preparing to start a new Lifetime movie. Because our jobs have us in different locations, the drives to the airport when it is time for one of us to depart are not the most uplifting. As a matter of fact, I will boldly step out and say, we both are guilty for sitting in an element of sadness, anxiety, or frustration, because one of us is leaving the other. Obviously, when we are driving to pick up the other, the emotion is much different! It is uplifting, exciting, and a lot of happiness leading up to it.

Those departures though, whew, they have the ability to send us in a spiral … of negative feelings and emotions. Now, back to this day. I woke up, stretched my arms out, and said to myself, "Today is the day I will bring joy!" I thought this could be a total game changer for us. If I woke eager and excited for the day, all the way through, and my husband saw my spirit, then this will be a positive for him, especially since he was the one departing.

I truly did it!

All day, even at the airport, I was enthused to see him on his way. For the first time, I left the airport Departure terminal, joyful! I was happy my entire commute home (leaving the Washington, DC area is not a fun journey). I analyzed the situation on my way home, and even thought to myself, *How am I so happy right now?* Normally, this would be a sad or frustrating drive. Typically, I would be left feeling lonely and sad.

What it boiled down to on that day, was that the spirit I chose to be in, all day long, was positive. I chose and even chased JOY! When I got home, I decided to finish writing this piece on joy. Even more astonishing on how the Lord works: my husband sent me a scripture from the gate at the airport within an hour of me dropping him off for the first time with my new joyful spirit and heart.[38] Looking at that scripture, I was so blessed that my joy brought him joy also.

Whether a college football fan or not, Dabo Swinney interviewed after the Clemson victory in 2019 said, "For me, joy comes from focusing on Jesus, others, and yourself." Every time I focus on joy now, I think of that statement. It will always be impactful to me.

Much like the mountains that have been majestically created for us by our creator, life will have peaks and valleys throughout, and there will be ups and downs, but ultimately how we choose to receive our blessings and focus on joy is completely up to us.

38. Proverb 17:22-18:2

We are Equipped

Vickie Hall

Growing up, I would admire my mom and think, *I can't wait to be a grown up.* I wanted a husband, family, job, house, car, and the freedom to do what I wanted, when I wanted to do it. It seemed so glamorous to me.

She made it look easy.

Little did I know at the time was with all of that, comes responsibilities. Now that I am a wife, mother, have a job, house, and a car, it's not so easy. There isn't much freedom.

When I was asked to contribute to this

book, the first thing that came to mind was how women are able to manage the day-to-day without appearing overwhelmed. I have witnessed it time and time again throughout the years. I cannot explain it logically. However, I do believe that God made us this way. He made us to be nurturers, pillars of support, compassionate, multi-taskers, organized (even organized chaos), and emotionally capable.

As I look back through my life's journey, I am amazed at God's grace in what I've been through. We all have a story to share. I have learned that even though there will always be someone who has "been through worse," it doesn't mean what I am going through isn't difficult. I have learned over the last five years, more than ever, that it is okay to admit that life is hard at times and that often I am simply going through the motions. There isn't a need to diminish the truth or soften the blow.

Five years ago, my husband, Jim, started having severe pain in his neck. He had an MRI and was told that his vertebrae were damaged and compressing the nerves. He tried physical therapy as instructed, and the pain continued to worsen. He had surgery shortly thereafter. The neurosurgeon fused four vertebrae. It was no doubt a big surgery, and his recovery was brutal. In the fifteen years of marriage, this was my first experience as a caregiver and dealing with my spouse having a major physical issue. This wasn't like him having the flu for a week. He even had to learn how to swallow again. I'd help him to the bathroom and in and out of bed. I made a spreadsheet with all of his medicines and tracked when he took them. He couldn't lift, bend, twist, reach, or drive. My sons, Brandon and Nathan, were troopers. Between the three of us, we took care of business!

He went back to work six months later. Whew! We made it through the prior ten months. During that time, we went to his check-ups every three months. After a year, the neurosurgeon said it was all fused and looked good. The problem was that Jim continued to have pain, though he was about 75 percent better. His doctor said to give it another six months. He did that, but the pain continued. Not only did the physical pain continue for him, but the emotional pain for our family did as well. Seeing him in so much distress every day was indescribable. The impact that it was having on our family dynamic became apparent with each passing day. He was only able to manage the pain at night by medication, and that really isn't pain management. His patience was thin with the boys, and many times you could cut the tension in our house with a knife. We continued to walk on egg shells, smiled, loved him, supported him, and did everything we could to help him.

I stayed in good spirits and recognized "in sickness and in health" from our marriage vows was not a phrase to be taken lightly. I was committed to doing whatever I could to get him and our family through this time. I kept repeating myself over and over again to the boys, "Just be patient. This is temporary. We will get through this." Meanwhile, life continued, and the world did not stop spinning. Between work, raising teenagers, and family life, the days would come and go. Family and friends would ask how everything was going, and I'd say, "Fine." I'm not sure why, but I felt like it was a bad thing to say otherwise.

My life was "fine."

Overall, I still felt so blessed, and I did not ever want to come across as complaining. I would feel guilty.

Next thing you know, I was laid off for the first time in twenty years of working from a job that I thought I would retire from. I loved the company and people I worked with for almost fourteen years. The company was sold to a larger company, and that was all she wrote. I took the holidays and additional time off, and then moved on to finding a new job. It was such a different experience searching for a job. Everything was electronic, and I had to make sure I had key words included in my résumé and signed up on all the internet job search engines. I accepted a new position and was excited for a new endeavor.

Life continued. One day, I received a call at work from Jim, who told me Brandon's school had called, and he had been attacked. My heart dropped. Everything in my body went cold and numb. I thought, *My son was physically harmed at school.* He had a mild concussion. I took a deep breath and said, "Thank God he is okay. I will meet you at home." I didn't cry. I didn't rant. I didn't speed. I finished what I was working on, shut down my computer, and drove home. Within days, we met with the principal, sheriff's office, and started researching private schools. School tours and shadow days were scheduled within two weeks, and we were registered with a new school for the next school year for both boys. Brandon did not want to return to school for the last nine weeks. We continued to support him, but of course, also encouraged him to push through.

I was talking with Brandon one evening; it was a good and long conversation. He started fidgeting and looking down. I asked him what was wrong, "You can tell Momma anything." He began to weep and started blurting out some of his deep feelings. I could not believe what I was hearing. He thought possibly our life could be better without him.

How could he think the world may be better if he wasn't in it?

He and his brother are our world. There are not enough words I can use to express my feelings and emotions as I listened to his hurt and saw him break down. He went on to explain that he did not know what his purpose was in life. He told me that he did not think about hurting himself or taking his own life, but was having so many different thoughts running through his mind. He was down. At the time, he was only fourteen. We got him the help and after one of his sessions his counselor said, "Hang in there, Momma. You are the calm in the storm."

I showed up to work one morning, and my supervisor came in to speak with me. He said the owner expected each department to have a list ready for a lay-offs since they were not doing well financially. He continued to say that the other employee in our legal department had been with him for twenty-five years, so it would be me. He recommended I start looking for a job and wanted to give me the professional courtesy.

Really? I thought.

I took a deep breath and thanked him for letting me know. People always say that God will not give us more than we can handle, but again, "Really?" Just another thing to add to my list.

Bring it on, I thought.

The job search started again … and so did the diarrhea!

You heard me!

I went to work every day not knowing if that would be my last day, while searching for a job and interviewing, taking care of the household, dealing with my husband being in pain, working through Brandon's emotions, making sure Nathan was okay, extracurricular activities, and trying to maintain my family and friend relationships.

I told myself often, "Suck it up, buttercup!"

I found a job soon after. When I went to resign, it seemed like they were shocked. Things were looking up for the company, and they said they wished I would stay. Needless to say, I had to move forward.

It was a different environment at the new job, but it was a paycheck. I got settled, had a performance evaluation, and received a raise. Six months after I started, I was laid off.

No, I am not joking! I was laid off three times in only eighteen months.

I received a nice severance and felt fortunate. I know everything happens for a reason. I decided to take plenty of time to search for a new job and ultimately decided to change industries. The Oil and Gas industry was too volatile. I declined job offers and continued to search.

During that period, Jim had to have a second neck surgery, after the pain got so bad he would cry on his knees. I realized it was a blessing to be laid off, as I was able to take care of him for another six months.

Words are not sufficient enough to explain witnessing the person you love so dearly continue to be in pain, and there is nothing you can do to take it away. That time was more difficult than the first surgery. The mental and emotional strain on him was tremendous, as well as for our family. God knew what He was doing by having me home. I will never forget the look in my husband's eyes when he came home from work early one day. He looked at me and said, "I do not know what I would have done had you not been at home today. I can now understand where people believe the only option is taking their own life when nothing else is helping." We cried together, and cried some more. Then, he went on to get the counseling and help he desperately needed.

Fast forward to today. Jim's pain has continued to increase. There are times when I felt like everyone and everything around me were crumbling. It has been five years since this began. Throw everything else into the mix, and I can honestly say it has been extremely difficult.

I am not embarrassed to say it anymore.

It has been the most challenging time in my forty-five years on earth. I have remained faithful, patient, supportive, and mostly positive, but no longer naïve to the reality we all face in our life's journey. Our marriage and family have been tested throughout these five years. Many tears have been shed, and all the egg shells are broken now. At one point, I told Jim that this could destroy our marriage if we allowed it to. However, I would do everything I could for that not to happen.

Jim has guilt for his personality, attitude,

sensitivity, and demeanor that have changed due to the pain. There is also memory loss. He is working through those emotions. Jim before the pain started and Jim after the pain started are different people. We have all endured a lot and are closer than ever because of it. I keep reminding myself and the boys that five years is nothing compared to the next thirty-five to come.

We all ride the roller coaster of life.

There are ups, downs, and all arounds.

We were made to be the threads that keep a family or relationships together and strong.

During tough times, remember that you are well-equipped as a wife, mother, friend, co-worker, and family member. You have everything you need to handle any situation or season, and you will be able to do it with God's Grace. You will look back on these situations or seasons and be amazed at what you can survive.

It is often in the fire that we learn what we are made of.

Keep in mind that remaining faithful doesn't mean you cannot feel hurt or discouragement. Your faith is what will help you through those times, so that you do not remain there.

Lean on your family and friends. The people

who love you do want to be there for you, just as you want to lift them up. Most loved ones feel honored to pray for and support you.

Most important to remember is that you've got this!

My boys started calling me "Super Woman." Each day, I am grateful I wake up. And each day, I take a few moments to imagine what color cape I will wear to match my outfit!

What color is your cape today?

Willing

Emily Smith

"Emily Michelle! Little ladies don't talk that loud!"

I've always been loud and outspoken. Some of my earliest memories include being shushed by my mother. Also, adding frequently to general conversation that I talked too much in school. Now, though, I can look back over my life and connect the dots. I see God's handiwork in creating me to be who He has called me to be. Little did I know that as an adult, my voice would be heard for such a time as this.

On Mother's Day in 2012, I wasn't surprised by this news that I had a mass in my brain. I had been having voracious headaches for a couple of weeks. I really just wanted everyone to leave and turn off the light. I leaned back on the bed and put a towel over my face thinking it would help with the pain. My husband, Jason, and I patiently waited for the on-call doctor to pay us a visit. We should've been in church celebrating, but instead we awaited plans for moving forward with a brain tumor. Although the tension was thick in that emergency room that Sunday morning, I had never experienced more peace. A peace I couldn't even understand.

Have you ever prayed the prayer, "God, use me. I want to be your vessel?" I laugh when I say be careful what you pray for, because He just might do that in the most unexpected ways!

The next several hours and days are still a blur. After the initial CT scan that revealed the tumor, we had to make a plan. The neurologist was adamant; the tumor had to come out. The doctor gave a date for surgery, however, in my mama-mind, I knew that was impossible. It was the end of the school year, there was a school luau to attend, as well as an awards day. I could not miss these special events with my children, no matter the pain or the urgency.

Needless to say, the doctor relented on his first date of operation and agreed upon Friday. We needed to move forward quickly, he'd said.

Friday morning came along with all of the emotions you can imagine. Brain surgery is a scary thought! But through it all, I had been standing on the promise of Psalm 91.[39] I repeated this several times a day, prayed it constantly, and rested in God's faithfulness to cover me throughout the whole process. The most afraid I ever felt during this whole process, was when they wheeled me away from my family to enter surgery. I knew I wasn't alone, that God was with me, but I also knew I was headed into the complete and utter terrain of the unknown. The unknown is scary. Especially when you can't see the whole path in front of you.

Surgery ended, and all was well. One of the first of many miracles during my stent with cancer would happen here. The surgeon told us to expect a six-to-eight-hour surgery. Imagine my husband's surprise when the doctor called after just two hours later and said they were finished. The doctors were able to get the entire tumor, and I was cleared with "clear margins."

The second miracle of this operation would be that I did not need a head harness to support my head and neck. Jason said that was one of the hardest times for him and my mama was preparing to walk in to see me after surgery. They weren't sure what they would find. Again, he was met with total surprise when he walked into the ICU to see me sitting up in my bed without a harness. God was surely showing us His faithfulness in our desperate time of need. I spent three days in ICU then moved into a regular room.

Only two weeks after surgery, I was shopping with my mom when Jason called and said I needed to get home. I was a bit aggravated, because our time was getting cut short. I asked him what was wrong as I could hear the tension in his voice. He simply replied that I needed to get home quickly. Again, true to "Emily style" I told him I couldn't come immediately, as I *needed* to pick up our youngest from his friend's house. Jason reiterated "Emily, come home now." It's odd really, but I think I knew what was coming. I mentally prepared myself as we drove home and prayed, believing God was in complete control, and I was still healed.

When I walked in, Jason was standing in the kitchen looking pale.

"The nurse called with your results. It's cancer," he said.

I'd like to say that I reacted, but I didn't.

I stood there, numb. I don't think one is ever fully prepared to hear the words, "You've got cancer." I was reminded of the emergency room and the complete peace that washed over me. I knew this was a pivotal moment in this cancer journey I was forced into. Still, I chose to believe. I chose to believe God at His Word when He said He would cover me and be my shield and rampart. I chose to believe when God whispered words of healing. I chose to believe my life was not over.

The following fifteen months entailed seventeen rounds of chemotherapy and other treatments. Through it all, God sustained me. If I learned anything, it was this: God is good even in the bad. God is not a God of sickness and disease. God uses *all* things for the good of his people if we will allow Him.[40]

Would I, had I been asked beforehand, have been willing to go through this? I'd like to think I would've, but truth is, I wouldn't have been willing. Now that I am on the other side, my faith having been built through trusting God, I am ready to hand it all over to Him daily. I am also willing to help show the world His Peace.

All He needs is for me to be a willing vessel.

39. Psalm 91:4
40. Proverbs 3:5-6

Take 63

Elizabeth Collums

Years ago, when my youngest daughter graduated from Southeastern University in Hammond, Louisiana, the commencement speaker shared these words of wisdom, "Don't forget who packed your parachute." In other words, you didn't get here on your own. Landing into adulthood, with a degree in-hand, was the mixture of many steady, helping hands, whether directly or indirectly.

I was proud as everyone there that we all somehow had a part in the nurturing and supporting roles we played as each name was called out during the ceremony. I'm also sure that there were many parents missing and had been missing out for quite some time. Grandparents, aunts, uncles, foster parents, and friends have (since the beginning of time) had to step up and stand in the gap to raise children.

As I drove away that evening, I thought heavily on who packed mine and just how many parachutes does one need in a lifetime? When I was growing up, I somehow felt that it was up to me to nurture myself. My parents were not the sort that cared about my emotional or mental state or even if I had the capacity for one. Even so, I am thankful that I had a bed to sleep in, food to fill my stomach, and permanent shelter. Our house was old and tattered, but it was ours. If it had not been for the caregivers of the world, it would have been a difficult fall, because I had been cared for and nurtured when I wasn't looking, by those outside my home.

During the '70s, we all grew up in a no nonsense, do-your-homework-or-you-get-an-F era. Albeit, none of us graduated on the level of scientists, computer geeks, or white collar professionals. We all worked out of the same box of 64 colors, and I thank God for that every day.

We all came from the same economic and social backgrounds. Nobody gave a wit about name brands or what model car you drove. We all dressed in blue jeans, t-shirts, tennis shoes, or whatever. I honestly can't remember anyone being mocked, teased, or made fun of for what you wore to school or what kind of car you drove. Someone was almost always available to give me a ride if I needed one, and we often shopped for something new to wear in one another's closet.

Our teachers were old, young, male, female, white, and black, and they filled the much-needed role of not only being teachers and testers but investors in our future. They were tough and none-too-eager to please. That was not their job. Their job was to call us to attention and respect the speaker whether we agreed or not. They taught us English, civics, the wonderful history and geography of this great country, and all the others that make up the world map. We learned math, science, art, typing, foreign languages, welding, automotive repair, typing, and many other electives. I remember mouthing off a bit to my typing teacher that I'd probably never need typing, and she point blank told me that, "You never know what you're gonna need one day."

And she was right.

All those so-called "wasted days and weeks" on things we thought we would never need or use, did matter. I can honestly say I have used those skills taught to me nearly every day of my life since. And I can still, to this day, see Mrs. Lewis walking between the rows of our desks as we reluctantly pounded away on our typewriters.

We learned about community service in the Beta Club, and we honed our social skills at pep rallies, recess periods, school sporting events, and dances. We learned how to be creative as we turned our gyms into winter wonderland for homecoming games with poster boards, colored paper, disco balls, and confetti.

And this was all because of teachers, who not only were committed in the classrooms, but gave their time for before and after school events. How many teachers packed your parachute? I can just about say all of mine. Don't get me wrong. I didn't like many of them. At the time, I thought they were mean, frank, stern, and had that look in their eyes that could burn a hole right through you. But, they showed up every day and plowed through the next chapter or the next lesson until you got it.

I had other teachers as well. Those were the most dedicated of all. They were my Sunday school teachers. For they were paid nothing and given little praise for their dedication, time, and preparation. They showed up whether the room was filled on Easter Sunday or only a few of us during the summer. We were taught lessons from throughout the Bible about Noah's Ark, Moses, and the Israelites with all the miracles that preceded their escape from the Egyptians. The unforgettable stories of Jonah and the whale, the healing of the leper, and all the inspiring events and promises from the Bible that gave me the internal hope that I so desperately needed. So, even though I felt my parents lacked the know-how or ability to fill my heart, I'm thankful that my mom knew where to go each and every Sunday so I could get it.

Most of us in the 70805 zip code barreled straight into the work force, eager to make that first paycheck. Maybe our expectations would be considered low by today's standards, but we were proud, excited, and embolden to be out in the world and on our own. We would rent a bit, scrape enough cash together for that first 1,200 square-foot house, and we felt like we hit the lottery. Maybe marry, have a couple children, move up into a three-bedroom, two-bath and you'd just pinch yourself. I listen every day to the discontent in people's lives as I drive past newly-developed, oversized homes on oversized lots. The town I live in has dozens of storage facilities full of overflow.

Why? When is enough ever going to be enough?

For those reading this, the wisdom I can give you is this: those things are not the things meant to fill our children's parachutes. The need for the accumulation of things and possessions only reinforces the wrong kind of success in life.

I've worked in the healthcare industry, insurance and utility companies, law offices, and the postal service. I've had managers, supervisors, and employers that have treated me well and those who have not. I had the privilege of working for, and underneath, men and women who had the most diligent work ethic and never once took advantage of their positions of authority. I've had others that, at that moment in time, made the devil look like a minor league player.

As we have all experienced, I've made more than my share of wrong turns and suffered the consequences each and every time. Ah, and lest we not forget those insurmountable uphill battles doing it alone, or so I thought. Every consequence delivered along with every uphill battle was part of the growing process of what "works" and what doesn't. In other words, the many doors that God has closed and opened. And, I have to say that my parachute has been filled up on many occasions from some of the wisest and most elegant women I've ever met. Their advice was never long-winded, but short and succinct "quotable notables."

"Dear, you're not crazy. The people you are hanging around with are. You need to find new friends."

"A good man is already doing the right thing when you meet him. Don't waste your time waiting to see if he will."

"When somebody shows you their true colors, you better believe it the first time. Don't make them keep showing you over and over again," and my all time favorite was, "If you keep looking back, you're just going to fall again. You just need to name it, claim it, ask for forgiveness, and move on."

You see, if you think about it, we're all in this together. The packing of parachutes, that is. We have so many stages in our lives that we have to start anew. Rebirthings can come at any stage in our lives. And with each new beginning, we all have experienced fear, doubt, and wobbly legs. And yet, God is always there. Not just standing and watching, but sending the right people our way at the right time if we just ask. The parachutes of life are what save us, but where and when we jump is what makes us.

I've lived a pretty unremarkable, slow, but steady life. And as this New Year began, I faced retirement after forty-five years in the workforce. I've been touched by so many good and kind people who are no longer here for me to thank and many who meant to destroy me that I still struggle to pray for. But, ultimately, it was God that packed my parachute that day on the cross when he gave his life for me.

When the anxiety of what comes next hits me, this old girl is going to believe that story that was taught to me long ago. Moses sent twelve spies to explore the Promise Land and ten of those twelve showed little faith that it was right for them. Only Caleb and Joshua could see the land of milk and honey.

Our lives are what we make of them. I often have trouble verbally expressing myself. But put a pen in my hand, get my mouth out of the way, and my thoughts and feelings flow more freely.

I've published one book to date, *Passengers*. And again, this was with the help of yet another wise, kind, and encouraging woman.

I've been given nearly sixty-three years of God's grace and mercy along with opportunities to give and take every lesson learned on every jump.

The next one is not solely mine to make, as I have earnestly prayed for God to fulfill my heart's desire to be a writer. But, if this isn't his plan for me, then something more fulfilling and meaningful will be packed in my parachute, I'm sure of it.

Quiet

Yvette Whittington

The loudest sound I ever heard was the quiet. Absolutely nothing. No pitter patter of feet, no giggles from the back of the house, just silence. It was amazing how quiet my house became when my children moved out. And yet, it is the loudest sound I think my ears will ever hear. Your house goes from doors shutting, blow dryers roaring, and music blaring, to absolute, unrestful silence.

I remember living in three rooms in my house once my daughters were gone: the kitchen, the bedroom, and the restroom. I didn't walk down the hall or into the back rooms at all after that day. I no longer sat in the living room; there was no more living in that house. It was just a room—a cold, lonely room. There's always a certain level of worry when your kids move out. You pray they will make good, sound decisions. You hope you have prepared them for a world that often has no mercy.

And you silently pray to yourself that you, too, can survive letting them go.

After all, for so long it had been just the three of us. For the most part, there will never be a soul more forgiving, more understanding, and willing to give you a second, third, and fourth chance than a mother. And when someone hurts your kids, they hurt you. Before you know it, the mama bear is out in protection mode. Personally, I always had a hard time standing my ground with anyone, until someone hurt my daughters.

I was the mother that wanted to prevent their child's mistakes from occurring; I didn't want them to go through the pain of what one wrong decision could cause. My youngest was the hardest to let go. I couldn't for the life of me look at her and see a young woman; I still saw my little blond-headed girl with pig tails holding onto my leg for security, crying, begging me not to leave her. And then, I found myself holding onto her for selfish reasons, to be honest.

I wasn't ready to let her go.

I knew I couldn't beg or plead with her to stay. The day she was set to move, I resigned to my room, closing the door behind me, as they removed the last of her belongings from our home. I felt like someone was ripping my heart out. After all, that was my little girl.

That was also the last day that house was a home to me.

From that point on, it was four walls—just a shell of a home. I can remember the first three years of her being gone; I continued to lecture her, stressing the importance of being dependable and responsible. Only, there I was, still holding on and trying to control what she did. I would be up late at night wondering if she had everything she needed. *Was she eating? Was she being taken care of?* I was so obsessed with these thoughts, they consumed me. I couldn't sleep at night, and found I was easily distracted at work. When I did talk to her, I came off as mad or controlling. When in reality, it was more worry than anything. I don't really remember the dynamics with my own mother, so it's hard for me to relate with my daughter and how upset she gets when I am constantly badgering her.

One would have thought I was in the final stages of dying, trying my hardest to make sure she was safe and that she would be okay without me.

But I was, simply put, just having a hard time letting go. I promised myself silently that once she was married I would let go, that I would lean into my new role as her mother-friend, instead of mother-disciplinary. I no longer needed to be teacher, but rather the encourager. It was important for both of us that I embrace my new role; she needed me to just be there for the good, the bad, and everything inbetween. She didn't need to be told what to do or what she'd done wrong.

And when the day came, as I walked her down the aisle, with each step, I let go a little more. As I gave her away in those last moments, so many things flashed before my eyes. Her as a child smiling up at me with those pretty blue eyes, thinking I was her world, to now, her watching her future husband and seeing her entire world.

I stood watching my little girl become this beautiful young woman, so kind and sincere. She makes me so proud to be her mom-friend;

her heart is good, and her soul is beautiful.

I remember letting go of my oldest daughter's hand as I walked her to first day of her kindergarten class. She wasn't the slightest bit concerned that I was leaving her there with all these strangers. She hugged my neck, waved bye, and off she went. She studied and did her homework independently. I never had to stay on top of her and push her; she pushed herself. I remember thinking, years later, how I missed out on her being just the least bit dependent on me. How I never had to sit down and do spelling words or math problems with her; it all came so easy to her. Fast forward, twenty years later, walking her down the aisle to her soon-to-be husband, was such a different experience than it was with my youngest. She was so beautiful, so sure of who she was, confident and independent, but still always my girl. I knew, on each of their wedding days, I wasn't the one they envisioned taking that walk down the aisle with, and I was okay with that.

The year prior to both my daughters' weddings was especially hard, full of heartache for them, with the unexpected loss of their father in a house fire. They were both broken, and there was nothing I could do to fix their pain. Me, their protector for their entire lives, could do nothing to lessen the hurt. As I sat on that front row of the funeral home, holding on to my daughters crying, one on each shoulder, I could feel the pain radiating from them. The brokenness was almost unbearable. Watching your children hurt and not being able to console them is torture. I remember my youngest daughter holding on to me, burying her head on my shoulder, and crying out. It was the hardest thing I have ever had to watch them go through, and I couldn't make it better.

With both of their wedding plans commencing not long after, the emotions of not having a father to walk them down the aisle would soon take over. I knew what they were feeling, but knowing it would have not been of any comfort to say that to them. I could only listen and do my best to be there for them. I knew this would be an emotional time, and I was very honest with them as I said, "You will never get over the loss of your father, but I can promise you it will get better, easier to deal with. The overwhelming sense of sadness will weigh heavy on your heart; you won't be able to focus on anything but this for some time. It will be hard to go to work. Hard to do much of anything. You will get mad, sad, and confused, sometimes within a matter of minutes. But one day, you will wake up, and the tears will begin to slow down. They will go from every hour to every four, to every day, to every other day, but your thoughts of him will never disappear. You will find yourself forgetting his face and his voice at times. And the first time you smile or laugh, you will feel guilty. You will ask yourself how can you smile knowing your dad is no longer here. You will often ask, 'Do the people around me not know what happened?' and you will feel hurt by that. Then, one day, you will smile when you think of him, and you will realize that you have arrived to a peaceful place. You will never just get over it. There will be some days in the years to come that certain moments will happen, and you will wish he was there. And you'll cry. Or a certain smell out of nowhere will remind you of him. And you'll cry." I know, because I go through it with my own dad.

I talked to God a lot. I told Him that whatever hurt my girls have or when they needed to cry out in pain or frustration, turn them my way Lord. Please turn them my way. Give me the wisdom and the strength to say what is needed to help them. Give me the words needed to comfort them Lord; they are only turning to me because they know I will be here. No matter what, I will be there.

Then, it was time to plan the weddings. I was so excited, I could see happiness creep its way back in. The excitement it brought gave them a much-needed break from the pain; it became therapy for them. And my heart filled with joy as I watched them smile again. When news that my oldest daughter was pregnant came, I was so happy. God knew my daughters, both of them, needed this child. They needed a renewing.

I was sitting with loved ones in the waiting area, ready for my grandson to make his arrival, when my youngest daughter came and told me that my oldest daughter wanted me with her for the birth. I teared up. My independent daughter needed me. I was so blessed to be the first person to hold my grandson, more blessed to have been there with my daughter.

That birth was a new start for both of my daughters, one as his mother, and another as his aunt.

And for me, as a mother, to both of them.

Being a mother is challenging at any age, but being a mother to adult daughters can be downright brutal. Women and girls are such emotional creatures; the dynamics between them can implode at any moment. You have to tread lightly at times, the "dark days" as I call them, will arrive. One day, she will go to bed your sweet, carefree child having said "I love you, Mom. You're the best." and the next, a stranger.

You'll find yourself asking, "Where is my child?" And then it'll hit you, she's not a child anymore. You'll learn to sit back and let them come to you. You'll watch them fall, and then they will get back up. You'll watch their successes and be proud of them.

I have a different role, not only for my daughters, but for my husband's kids—my bonus family comprised of a daughter, son, and all of their amazing spouses and children.

Life is simpler now. I, of course, still worry some days, but it's tolerable. Taking the time to slow down a bit as I get older, and realize that some of the things I worry and stress over are so minute. The relationships we have with those we love win over everything. That job you put so much time and effort into, no longer excites you, but helping your grandchild crack an egg for the first time does. And in the arms of your grandchildren, as they wrap around your neck, makes you the most important person in the world.

Moving from the mother-disciplinary phase, to the mother-friend phase is difficult, but you will be pleasantly surprised to find the best days are still ahead. They come in the whisper of children when they say, "I love you." They come in sitting on the front porch, holding hands with your best friend. With every twist in the road, every dark corner, and bended knee, you will one day realize the years you spent raising your children are such a short part of your life, and theirs, and you'll embrace the quiet place beautifully wrapped in memories. You'll look forward to the day you can retire and put that chapter behind you as well.

I look at my husband, my best friend, and I have peace. I hear the children or grandchildren laughing and watch as they all run from here to there, and my hope is that they all make it to this quiet, peaceful place one day. While all of the moments of my life count, I realize that each day, I am making the best memories yet.

Closing Letter

Tammi Arender

I woke recently with a real heaviness on my heart, an almost physical weight that settled on my chest. It was as though I could feel the gravity of everything I was going through. When that happens to me, I know in my heart that God is begging for my attention. He's wanting me to re-connect with Him. To reconnect with my family and friends. We spend so much time chasing things in life that simply don't matter.

God shouldn't have to beg.

We've become so infatuated with infatuation.

We want everyone and everything to bring us an immediate, emotional high. We'll do anything to get it. We'll medicate, manipulate, and negotiate with the devil. And that's when we start playing right into the devil's hands. He knows if we will give him the time of day, he'll get his little fungus-riddled toe in the door. Once that toe is even the tiniest bit inside, he knows he can, at some point, come rushing in. Because we, alone, can never beat him at his own game. He's the master at deceit and double-dealing. So it's up to us to not engage him in anyway. In the book of John, it says the enemy comes to steal, kill, and destroy.[41]

Those are some strong words. Nowhere in that statement do I see where the devil has my best interest at heart.

So why would I ever listen to him? Truth is, we don't often recognize Satan's attempts to get his tentacles in our business. It may be through food, people, power, or profession. Because those things, for a fleeting moment, can give us an infatuation sensation. It's human nature to want to be successful, liked, and looked at as someone who has it all together. However, having it "all together," may mean letting go of some person or habit that's holding us back from being what God wants us to be.

It's important to realize and recognize God as your source. Source of what?

Your source. Period.

Not just source of strength, joy, peace, and perseverance, but the source of the breath in your lungs. We're famous for wanting to give God our "spiritual side," but we want to hold on to our mental physical side. We want control. When truly, it's our mental and intellectual self that can be our biggest enemy. In 2 Corinthians, it says we can negate all arguments that are against the knowledge of God, and we take every thought captive to make us more obedient to Christ.[42]

That is so stinking hard to do! I get it. Every thought? Are you serious? Yes, ma'am … otherwise, we lose. We let the devil win the daily battle of the mind, instead of God. And what we focus on, we act on.

Thoughts become actions.

Actions, behaviors.

Behaviors, lifestyle.

I long for the time in my early Christian life when thinking about and dwelling on Jesus came easy. Wild horses couldn't keep me away from church or reading my Bible. I was like a kid at Christmas that had just gotten that long sought-after toy. It was mine. All mine.

I need to remember Jesus is ours. He's all ours, and He's all in. In every single thing we're going through. He's not on the outside looking in at us. He is with us, giving us the courage to fight the battle. But the discord comes when we won't allow God to fight that fight. We do not want to relinquish control. We think we know better than God.

But we don't.

I pray today that I'll listen to Him more. Focus on things that matter, not material things. Eternal things. People. Relationships.

Our society is hurting, broken, and just plain sick. Our selfishness sucks every bit of goodness out of us, unless we surrender our thoughts and actions to God.

Do you want to rid yourself of the heaviness? Sadness? Sickness?

I do.

I want to claim life and all its abundance every day.

Let's focus on Him and take the focus off of us. I used to work for a man who would say, "You'd be surprised how much you can get done when it doesn't matter who gets the credit."

If we stop looking for a pat on the back, that infatuation sensation, and give credit, honor and glory to Jesus, we will be surprised how quickly joy and peace enter our lives. How much more we get done. But it will take a daily effort to bring our every thought captive, and surrender our own will to His.[43]

I share these words with you not because I think I'm worthy to do so. I certainly am not. I've made terrible mistakes and missteps in my life. But I'm forgiven and just wanted to express what has been burning a hole in my heart recently.

I love you. I'm praying for each of you who read this. For all of us.

41. John 10:10
42. 2 Corinthians 10:5
43. 2 Chronicles 7:14

RESOURCES

In the United States there are 123 suicides per day.

An average of 44,965 suicides a year.

Only 1 in every 25 attempts are fatal.

Which means that in America alone, 1,124,125

people attempt to commit suicide each year.

Globally, 800,000 suicides are fatal every year, one every 40

seconds. Thought to be only 1 in every 20 attempts,

Which means around the world 16,000,000 people attempt to

commit suicide each year.

(American Foundation for Suicide Prevention and World Health Organization)

EVEN IF YOU DO NOT LIVE IN THE UNITED STATES, YOU CAN CALL ANY OF THESE HOTLINES FOR SUPPORT.

SUICIDE

Deciding to commit suicide doesn't happen overnight. It starts when a person adds death on their list of solutions to a problem, and it grows over months or years until death becomes the only viable option left in their mind. Someone you know, if not yourself, may be thinking today that suicide is your only option. If you feel it is, please seek help. You have nothing to lose but the pain.

Call The National Suicide Prevention Hotline:

1-800-273-TALK (8255)

Visit online:

www.suicidepreventionlifeline.org

SEXUAL ABUSE

Victims of physical and sexual abuse often times live with guilt and shame. Unfortunately, many never receive the help they deserve because of it. If you know someone, or if that someone is you, seek help today. I have seen firsthand the positive transformation that can happen in you or your loved one's life.

Call The National Sexual Assault Hotline:

1-800-656-HOPE (4673)

Visit online:

www.rainn.org

DOMESTIC ABUSE

Domestic abuse is one of the most underreported crimes. While many local authorities are taking this more seriously, it still remains one of the least prosecuted. If you need help, or know someone who does, please call the National Domestic Violence Hotline.

The website gives this notice on the home page: *Internet usage can be monitored and is impossible to erase completely. If you're concerned your internet usage might be monitored, call us at 800.799.SAFE (7233).*

Call The National Domestic Violence Hotline:

1-800-799-SAFE (7233)

Visit online:

www.thehotline.org

PARENTAL HELP

Parenting is overwhelming at times. We often times feel like we can share our frustration with others close to us for fear of feelings of failure. If you feel this way and need someone to talk to, please make the call.

The website, Operated by Parents Anonymous® Inc, states: *Being a parent is a critically important job, 24 hours a day. It's not always easy. Call the National Parent Helpline® to get emotional support from a trained Advocate and become empowered and a stronger parent.*

Call The National Parent Hotline:

1-855- 4A PARENT (427-2736)

Visit online:

www.nationalparenthelpline.org

APPENDIX

1   Be strong and courageous. Do not fear or be in dread of them, for it is the Lord your God who goes with you. He will not leave you or forsake you." Deuteronomy 31:6

2   So do not fear, for I am with you; do not be dismayed, for I am your God. I will strengthen you and help you; I will uphold you with my righteous right hand. Isaiah 41:10

3   Do not neglect to do good and to share what you have, for such sacrifices are pleasing to God. Hebrews 13:16

4   In their hearts humans plan their course, but the LORD establishes their steps. Proverbs 16:9

5   To everything there is a season, and a time to every purpose under the heaven. Ecclesiastes 3:1

6   And I have filled him with the Spirit of God, with wisdom, with understanding, with knowledge and with all kinds of skills, to make artistic designs for work in gold, silver and bronze, to cut and set stones, to work in wood, and to engage in all kinds of crafts. Exodus 31:3-5

7   A cheerful heart is good medicine, but a crushed spirit dries up the bones. Proverbs 17:22

8   Anxiety weighs down the heart, but a kind word cheers it up. Proverbs 12:25

9   God is in the midst of her; she shall not be moved; God will help her when morning dawns. Psalm 46:5.

10 When the righteous cry for help, the Lord hears, and

rescues them from all their troubles. Psalm 34:17

11 For I know the plans I have for you, declares the Lord, plans for welfare and not for evil, to give you a future and a hope. Jeremiah 29:11

12 And we know that in all things God works for the good of those who love him, who have been called according to his purpose. Romans 8:28

13 So teach us to number our days that we may get a heart of wisdom. Psalm 90:12

14 He did not retaliate when he was insulted, nor threaten revenge when he suffered. He left his case in the hands of God, who always judges fairly. 1 Peter 2:23

15 A hot-tempered person stirs up conflict, but the one who is patient calms a quarrel. Proverbs 15:18

16 A quarrelsome wife is like the dripping of a leaky roof in a rainstorm; restraining her is like restraining the wind or grasping oil with the hand. Proverbs 27:15-16

17 Above all else, guard your heart, for everything you do flows from it. Proverbs 4:23

18 A fool gives full vent to his anger, but a wise person holds it in check. Proverbs 29:11

19 I will give you a new heart and put a new spirit in you; I will remove from you your heart of stone and give you a heart of flesh. Ezekiel 36:26

20 Faithful are the wounds of a friend, but deceitful are the kisses of an enemy. Proverbs 27:6

21 Death and life are in the power of the tongue: and they that love it shall eat the fruit thereof. Proverbs 18:21

22 Jesus looked at them and said, "With man this is impossible, but with God all things are possible." Matthew 19:26

23 Blessed is she who believed that the Lord would fulfill His promise to her. Luke 1:45

24 So then we pursue the things which make for peace and the building up of one another. Romans 14:19

25 As iron sharpens iron, so one person sharpens another. Proverbs 27:17

26 A troublemaker plants seeds of strife; gossip separates the best of friends. Proverbs 16:28

27 A gossip goes around telling secrets, but those who are trustworthy can keep a confidence. Proverbs 11:13

28 A friend is always loyal, and a brother is born to help in time of need. Proverbs 17:17

29 Two are better than one, because they have a good return for their labor: If either of them falls down, one can help the other up. But pity anyone who falls and has no one to help them up. Also, if two lie down together, they will keep warm. But how can one keep warm alone? Though one may be overpowered, two can defend themselves. A cord of three strands is not quickly broken. Ecclesiastes 4:9-12

30 Therefore do not worry about tomorrow, for tomorrow will worry about itself. Each day has enough trouble of its own. Matthew 6:34

31 Blessed is the one who perseveres under trial because, having stood the test, that person will receive the crown of life that the Lord has promised to those who love him. James 1:12

32 Some time later the brook dried up because there had been no rain in the land. Then the word of the LORD came to him: "Go at once to Zarephath in the region of Sidon and stay there. I have directed a widow there to supply you with food." So he went to Zarephath. When he came to the town gate, a widow was there gathering sticks. He called to her and asked, "Would you bring me a little water in a jar so I may have a drink?" As she was going to get it, he called, "And bring me, please, a piece of bread."

As surely as the LORD your God lives," she replied, "I don't have any bread—only a handful of flour in a jar and a little olive oil in a jug. I am gathering a few sticks to take home and make a meal for myself and my son, that we may eat it—and die."

Elijah said to her, "Don't be afraid. Go home and do as you have said. But first make a small loaf of bread for me from what you have and bring it to me, and then make something for yourself and your son. For this is what the LORD, the God of Israel, says: 'The jar of flour will not be used up and the jug of oil will not run dry until the day the LORD sends rain on the land.'"

She went away and did as Elijah had told her. So there was food every day for Elijah and for the woman and her family. For the jar of flour was not used up and the jug of oil did not run dry, in keeping with the word of the LORD spoken by Elijah.

Some time later the son of the woman who owned the house became ill. He grew worse and worse, and finally stopped breathing. She said to Elijah, "What do you have against me, man of God? Did you come to remind me of my sin and kill my son?"

"Give me your son," Elijah replied. He took him from her arms, carried him to the upper room where he was staying, and laid him on his bed. Then he cried out to the LORD, "LORD my God, have you brought tragedy even on this widow I am staying with, by causing her son to die?" Then he stretched himself out on the boy three times and cried out to the LORD, "LORD my God, let this boy's life return to him!"

The LORD heard Elijah's cry, and the boy's life returned to him, and he lived. Elijah picked up the child and carried him down from the room into the house. He gave him to his mother and said, "Look, your son is alive!"

Then the woman said to Elijah, "Now I know that you are a man of God and that the word of the LORD from your mouth is the truth." 1 Kings 17:7-24

33 Is anyone among you in trouble? Let them pray. Is anyone happy? Let them sing songs of praise. Is anyone among you sick? Let them call the elders of the church to pray over them and anoint them with oil in the name of the Lord. And the prayer offered in faith will make the sick person well; the Lord will raise them up. If they have sinned, they will be forgiven. Therefore confess your sins to each other and pray for each other so that you may be healed. The prayer of a righteous person is powerful and effective.

Elijah was a human being, even as we are. He prayed earnestly that it would not rain, and it did not rain on the land for three and a half years. Again he prayed, and the heavens gave rain, and the earth produced its crops. James 5:13-18

34 You intended to harm me, but God intended it for good to accomplish what is now being done, the saving of many lives. Genesis 50:20

35 Therefore do not worry about tomorrow, for tomorrow will worry about itself. Each day has enough trouble of its own. Matthew 6:34

36 And the peace of God, which transcends all understanding, will guard your hearts and your minds in Christ Jesus. Philippians 4:7

37 But Sarah denied it, saying, "I did not laugh," for she was afraid. He said, "No, but you did laugh." Genesis 18:15

38 A joyful heart is good medicine, but a crushed spirit dries up the bones. Proverb 17:22-18:2

39 He will cover you with His feathers, and under His wings you will find refuge; His faithfulness will be your shield and rampart. Psalm 91:4

40 Trust in the Lord with all your heart, and do not lean on your own understanding. In all your ways acknowledge him, and he will make straight your paths. Proverbs 3:5-6

41 The thief comes only to steal and kill and destroy; I have come that they may have life, and all its abundance. John 10:10

42 We demolish arguments and every pretension that sets itself up against the knowledge of God, and we take captive every thought to make it obedient to Christ. 2 Corinthians 10:5

43 If my people, which are called by my name, shall humble themselves, and pray, and seek my face, and turn from their wicked ways; then will I hear from heaven, and will forgive their sin, and will heal their land. my people. 2 Chronicles 7:14

MIKELYN AMPHION

Mikelyn Amphion lives in Georgia and is a full-time student. She is also the author of the children's book, *The Great Life of Lou Lou*, which stems from her true rescue story with her dog, Lou Lou. She has previously lived in Louisiana and Tennessee. Mikelyn enjoys spending time with her family and loves being outdoors. Walking and hiking are some of her favorite activities.

TAMMI ARENDER

Tammi Arender is a news personality, TV host, reporter, and owner Taste of Tallulah, an online bakery. She enjoys riding horses and Harleys. She is also an actress and voice over artist. Tammi has worked for TV stations in Baton Rouge, Louisiana, Little Rock, Arkansas, Charleston, West Virginia and Nashville, Tennessee. Tammi currently lives in Nashville and is an anchor/reporter for RFD-TV.

AIMEE BENNETT

Aimee Bennett is a lifelong Louisiana resident. She's a single mother of two, learning to do life her own way. She gets paid to do what she loves, working at a preschool where the kids can always bring a smile to her face even on the worst of days. She enjoys camping, travelling, crafting, DIY projects, and is excited to see where life takes her next.

NICOLE BRICE

Nicole Brice is the owner of Nicole Brice Consulting, as well as a writer and U.S. Army Veteran. She is a music and fashion lover, writes for several publications, and is a collector of pop culture memorabilia. Nicole currently lives in Greenwell Springs, Louisiana with her husband of nearly eleven years and their two children.

KEELEY BROOKS

Keeley Brooks is an entertainment journalist, public relations representative, and jazz music artist manager. She is also a yoga instructor and yoga nidra facilitator focused on stress relief. She enjoys laughing and loves movies, music, animals, tattoos, her family, carrots, rainy days, and spending time with her husband. Keeley has a book set to be released in 2021.

ELIZABETH COLLUMS

Elizabeth Collums, pen name of Ann Purvis, is the author of the historical fiction novel, *Passengers*. It was originally released in 2018, and then re-released through Rope Swing Publishing in 2020, with a new reading group guide. Ann is a retired USPS employee and enjoys DIY home projects and reading. She has a new book coming out in 2022.

COLLEEN CRAIN

Colleen Crain is a real estate professional serving the Greater Baton Rouge area. She's been helping people find their way in her city for many years, first as a radio and television traffic reporter, then as a registered nurse. Colleen calls the Garden District home and is the proud mother of her lovely, amazing daughter.

BRITTANY EDWARDS

Brittany Edwards is a stay-at-home mother of four children, three girls and one boy. She is married and lives with her husband in Baton Rouge, Louisiana. She enjoys outdoor activities and DIY projects with her kids.

KRISTI WILLIAMS FONTENOT

Kristi Williams Fontenot is a columnist for the Louisiana lifestyle publication, *Modern Grace magazine*, and inspirational blogger. Kristi's first nonfiction book will debut in 2021. She lives in Central, Louisiana with her husband and five children. Together they run a family-owned business.

SHARON CARROLL GREEN

Sharon Carroll Green has been an insurance agent serving her community for over twenty years. She was born and raised in Louisiana and is mother to two amazing boys, a beautiful daughter-in-law, and two precious grandchildren. She loves spending time with her grandkids, going to the beach, and antique and thrift store shopping.

VICKIE HALL

Vickie Hall is the author of *Please Don't Divorce Me*, a guide to parents going through a divorce. She is married to the love of her life and best friend. She and her husband have two sons and currently live in Prairieville, Louisiana.

JOY MORROW HOLDEN

Joy Morrow Holden is a high school english teacher and lives with her husband of fifteen years. Together they have two sons who are active, challenging, and tons of fun. Joy enjoys being in nature, walking, reading, cooking, baking, and a good cup of chai.

MICHELLE JAMES

Michelle James is a case manager at a behavioral health center in Louisiana and previously worked for the Medicaid health system. She lives with her husband of ten years. Together they have four children, and five grandchildren. She loves to draw, write, and be with family.

ALEXIS RANEA JESTER

Alexis Ranea Jester is a photographer, journalist, freelance literary editor, and media consultant. This Louisiana native's passions lie with environmental health and social justice. They actively fight for equality and rights for all people. Alexis enjoys being in nature, thrift shopping, and being in the company of close friends and family.

MICHELLE JESTER

Michelle Jester is a writer, editor-in-chief, and public relations/media consultant. She is the author of eleven books including fiction, nonfiction, and children's books. She lives in Louisiana with her husband, high school sweetheart and retired Master Sergeant. Together they have a son, daughter, and daughter-in-law. Michelle wears a bracelet with a single yellow rubber duckie charm on it to remind her to enjoy the fun and happy things of life.

MARIAH JESTER-WISE

Mariah Jester-Wise is from New York and currently lives in Louisiana with her husband of six years. She enjoys dancing, drawing, graphic design, video games, hiking, and sports. Mariah loves animals, coffee, and going to the beach.

MARCIE KLOCK

Marcie Klock is an IT project manager specializing in U.S. Military contracts. In addition, she is a writer and works part-time for her husband's film company. She has been married for six years, currently lives in Virginia, and has one son.

BRANDI LEBLANC

Brandi LeBlanc is the owner and founder of Barbelle Beauty Fitness, LLC. She is a professional women's bodybuilder and Certified Personal Trainer Master Practitioner. She currently holds four nationally-qualifying championship titles in both Women's Physique and Figure Divisions. Brandi lives with her husband in Louisiana, and together they have seven children.

JACQUELINE MEIER

Jacqueline Meier is a high school computer teacher who lives with her husband in Ohio. Together they have five sons and two granddaughters. Jackie enjoys painting—watercolor, acrylic abstracts, landscapes, floral—and runs the art studio Cool Runnings Design.

LYNN PALLASKE

Lynn Pallaske is living her dream working at a bookstore. She is also a book blogger and reviewer. Lynn currently lives in Kansas. With eight years active duty and being an Army brat from the age of seven, she has lived in Washington, Hawaii, Maryland, Nebraska, New York, Vermont, Georgia, and Germany. Lynn loves reading and hanging out with her dog.

TIARA PURNELL

Tiara Purnell is a financial analyst and personal finance coach that teaches financial literacy through *365intheBlack*. She loves DIY projects and helping people meet their financial goals. Tiara currently resides in Louisiana.

SHERRY REAMER

Sherry Reamer is retired from the Louisiana Department of Labor. She served as a CASA volunteer, a voice in court for children who are going through the foster care system, for five years. Sherry is married, has three children, eight grandchildren, and six great-grandchildren with another on the way. She loves spending time with her husband and family, reading, playing chess, decorating her home, and traveling.

MACY RUSHING

Macy Rushing is an author and stay-at-home mom. She lives on a farm in Ethel, Louisiana with her husband of five years. Together they have three children. She enjoys fishing, traveling, and spending time with her family. Macy has three children's books set to be released over the next two years.

KAREN SCOTT

Karen K. Scott is a shipping technician and serves on the media team at her church. In addition, she is a board member of Fathers on a Mission. Karen currently lives in Louisiana and enjoys traveling, DIY projets, and spending time with family and friends.

SARA SIMONEAUX

Sara Simoneaux is in marketing at her current position for thirteen years and a regular contributor to *Modern Grace magazine*. She lives with her husband in Brusly, Louisiana. Together they have a son and daughter. Sara loves date nights, Sunday outings and vacations with her family, spending time with friends and family, and snuggling with her dogs. She also loves to read books, often staying up all night to finish a book in a day.

EMILY SMITH

Emily Smith is a life coach, public speaker, blogger, second grade teacher, and Bible study leader. She is a cancer survivor, and through that journey found purpose to help others know the peace of God through adversity. Emily lives with her husband and their two children in Southaven, Mississippi. She enjoys reading, writing, running, watching their sons play baseball, and lounging by the pool in the summer.

SHANNON ORY SMITH

Shannon Ory Smith is a legal secretary. She lives in Meadville, Mississippi with her husband of twenty-four years. Together they have one son. Shannon enjoys cooking, especially coming up with new dishes, writing, and spending time with her family. She has a book due to release early 2022.

MEGAN PAUL TAUNTON

Megan Taunton hosts a Christian lifestyle podcast and blog and is co-founder of Aiden's Light Foundation, in honor of her daughter, Aiden Hilie Taunton, who passed away at five years old after a two-year battle with DIPG. Megan is author of the book, *I Think I Want to See Jesus*, and has four additional books releasing in the next two years. She lives with her husband, two children, and all of their animals in Louisiana.

ERIN VAVASSEUR

Erin Vavasseur is a photographer bartender, and professional model. She lives in Baton Rouge, Louisiana with her husband of four years, and together they have a son. Erin loves cooking, reading, writing, and exploring nature with her husband and son.

TIA WADE

Tia Wade is a dance and violin teacher at the Centre for the Arts in Baton Rouge, Louisiana. She is also a manager at a local grocery store. Tia is engaged to be married in November 2021, and enjoys dancing, reading, singing, and teaching dance.

YVETTE WHITTINGTON

Yvette Whittington is an author of the novel, *The Toolbox*, with a second novel publishing in early 2022. In addition, she has worked at the same company as her husband, for almost twenty years. Together they live in in Louisiana and have four children and four grandchildren, with one the way. Yvette enjoys spending time with her family, working on handmade crafts, and of course, writing.

ACKNOWLEDGEMENTS

To all of the incredible, amazing women who came together to participate in this book with me, thank you for opening your hearts and sharing your life experiences. You each possess a beauty for other women that supersedes what we were taught in society.

This book is dedicated to my father, who believed in women and raised us to believe in them also. He was an activist in the best way by raising his daughters to be part of a future where we help further the individuality and purpose of other women. Also, to my superhero husband, who witnessed, at a young age, several women in his life be abused and neglected, you are such a support to me. Thank you for helping me follow my dreams!

Editing, graphic design, and marketing are always an undertaking; however for this book it was huge! It is tough to organize editing and marketing for one author, let alone thirty-three. However, as overwhelming as it was, it was also rewarding! To the editing and graphic design wonderwomen:

Taylor Voisin, you are not only like a daughter to me, but an amazing friend, as well as an incredible designer and editor. Thanks for catching all the format and random glyphs errors, as well as putting back some of the commas that we feared didn't belong. Deborah Dawn Hall, and Mallory at Tell It All Editing, thank you for all of your last minute addons and conference calls. We were all video editing way before it was cool ... or mandatory. To the "Cs," Claire and Cheryl, behind the start-up, Prefaces Designs, you are building something great up there; keep going (and slow down long enough to get that website up, dang it!)

Pexels.com and Pixabay.com are such wonderful, free photo databases for creative marketing. We want to thank all of the photographers who contributed to our overall marketing efforts, especially Adrienne Andersen, Daniela Constantine, and Karolina Grabowska for their style, which seemed to fit most in our overall marketing vibe. Also, to Amber Faust, Anastasia Zhenina, Anete Lusina, Anna Nekrashevich, Asya Vlasova, Daria Shevtsova, Ena Marinkovic, Fallon Michae, Femke Defrère, Jess Bailey Designs, Jill Wellington, John Ray Ebora, Julia Larson, Leah Kelley, Lisa Fotios, Luis Quintero, Piotr Wróbel, Studio Layana, Taryn Elliot, Thought Catalog, Engin Akyurt, Anna Larin, DarkmoonArt_de, Yuri_B, Jill Wellington, dungthuyvunguyen, Perfecto_Capucine, hudsoncrafted, wanchun huang, Aliko Sunawang, and LaPorte. If I forgot anyone, I apologize and thank you also.

To God, my source of joy and peace, who gave me a dream and woke me at two in the morning with the title for this book and the cover. I am not a painter; however I pulled out all of my husband's supplies, prayed, and painted it ... all from that dream. God truly makes dreams come true; all He asks is for willing vessels.

Use us all, Lord.

—Michelle Jester

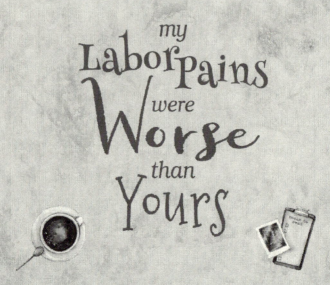

my Labor Pains were Worse than Yours

READING GROUP GUIDE

1. Have you ever caught yourself feeling incompetent because of the successes of women around you? Ever feel like you aren't good enough simply because you aren't as good at things other women are? Take a minute to digest that all women walk through the same feelings, and why finding your purpose for God and the world can help alleviate those feelings of unworthiness. (pgs 1-8)

2. Think on a situation where you've felt compelled to tell your story of trauma in defense of your own experience. Why do you think that you need to defend yourself or your experiences in front to others? Discuss better ways of finding your own validation for what you've been through and how you can use it to help others. (pgs 1-8)

3. Do you find you avoid social situations due to fear? What do you fear will happen? Do you often try to regulate things that are beyond your control? Or avoid things out of your control altogether? Discuss how this has affected your life in negative ways. What have you missed out on due to fear? (pgs 9-14)

4. Have you ever been in an abusive relationship, but stayed for reasons that you felt were more important than yourself? What was the reason you stayed and how does that decision feel to you now? (pgs 15-18)

5. Do you feel guilty about your past decisions? Do you feel you have let go of the guilt or do you still carry it with you? The reasons for guilt can vary, however take a minute to think on how you can release the baggage of your past by using it to help others, or by finding growth from it. (pgs 15-18)

6. What makes you uncomfortable in your own skin? What from your past caused you to feel this way? What steps can you take to unlearn the words that are seared into your psyche? For every one thing that makes you feel uncomfortable in your own skin list two things that you love about yourself. (pgs 19-22)

7. What broken path in your life caused you to change direction? Were you devastated by the change of course, or relieved? How do you feel about that change now? (pgs 23-33)

8. When you think of "family," who is sitting at your table? Are there times when your table felt empty? Reflect on who gave you a seat at their table and how that changed your life. (pgs 34-40)

9. What wrong, whether intentional or not, have you done to someone? What wrong has someone done to you? Is there anyone who has wronged you, and you feel you want to reach out to them? Why or why haven't you? If you have wronged someone else, what steps can you take to right that wrong? Does reflecting on how you've hurt others make you more understanding to those that have wronged you? (pgs 41-49)

10. What type of confrontation communicator are you? How can you better communicate with loved ones by knowing your own type? Did any of the other types remind you of others in your life? How do you think you can better communicate with them? (pgs 50-56)

11. What are your passions? How do you feel you can use your passions in the world around you? How

can you center a career around those passions? (pgs 57-60)

12. Do you live in the present, or are do you find yourself always looking back or forward? What things do you love to do that you've given up? Make a list of simple things that make you happy, and then set a course on doing them. (pgs 61-63)

13. Do you always chase the next relationship, be it romantic or platonic? What void do you think you have that needs to be filled? Take a minute to access the relationships that you've chased after. Did any of those fill the emptiness? Have you ever put God before those relationships and asked Him to help you? (pgs 64-69)

14. Have you experienced domestic violence from a parent or relative? Have you frozen in the face of violence committed against you? Do you feel guilt or responsibility for it? Do you see yourself as a victim or failure, or do you see yourself as a survivor? Make a list of all you've survived, and remind yourself that you've survived one hundred percent of your hardest days. (pgs 70-74)

15. Have you ever been made to feel you were not mentally fit? How has that affected the trust you have in your own decisions? Do you feel the people you surround yourself with have helped you, or have

they contributed to feelings of unworthiness? (pgs 75-89)

16. What situation in your life made you feel less-than or humiliated? How did you handle it? Do you feel that circumstance made you a better person? Discuss how or how not. (pgs 90-99)

17. How has gender double standards affected your development? Do you feel you are being the woman God created you to be, or someone else molded you to be? Reflect on a time you were "put in your place," and how it should have been different. (pgs 100-106)

18. How often do you feel talked over? Have you talked over other women in your life? How can you practice standing up for yourself and saying "I wasn't done talking," as well as recognizing when you do the same to others? (pgs 107-114)

19. Do you have a time where you didn't follow your own intuition and wish you had? What about the times that you did and are glad? Share how those times impacted your life. (pgs 115-121)

20. Who is your constant? It can be a friend, family member, partner, etc. (pgs 115-121)

21. Do you allow yourself the space to say no? How do you determine when it's healthy to say "no," and when it's healthy to say "yes?" (pgs 122-129)

22. Have you had to forgive someone close to you for something major they've done? Have you ever felt that so alone that you wanted to die? How would picturing them in a closet, crying and alone, and wanting to die help you forgive them? (pgs 122-129)

23. What was your metamorphosis stage of life? What was harder: having to reintroduce yourself to your loved ones, or reintroduce yourself to you? Do you feel like you lost yourself or do you feel like you gained a new self? (pgs 130-137)

24. Did you have people who were anchors that stood by you through your transition? Did you lose people and have to let others go? Reflect on the people who were anchors to you and the ones that wanted to know the new you. (pgs 130-137)

25. Ponder a time when you had to put away self-consciousness to get through a situation in your life. Was it in helping someone you loved, or in helping yourself? How did that experience help you to learn to face your self-doubt? (pgs 138-143)

26. Have you had a diagnosis of a child, parent, or sibling that was hard to deal with? Did you find other people who could help you understand the diagnosis and cope with the change it would bring? Have you since been that person to someone else? (pgs 144-152)

27. Have you experienced a situation where you were being abused, and a loved one knew about it but did nothing to help you? What reaction did that prompt in you? Do you think that you've found a purpose that came from having gone through it? (pgs 153-156)

28. Are there obstacles in your life that you feel you will never overcome? Do you feel like a failure because of them? How can changing your mindset to accept that some obstacles don't have to be overcome to become a positive, help you? Think of some of the obstacles in your life that you can count as successes by learning to use and control them, rather than get rid of them. (pgs 157-164)

29. Have you done something in the past that caused you to feel disgusted with yourself? Or found yourself in the same situation you'd talked down about others in the past for? Has someone else made you feel worthy and loved despite it? How can you use that experience to keep yourself from judging others? Loving others? (pgs 165-171)

30. Do you have special people in your life that you would miss terribly if they were gone? Have you lost loved ones that you wish you could go back and tell how much you love them? Take the opportunity to value the loved ones in your life, make a list of them, and find the time to spend with them while you still can. (pgs 172-176)

31. If you are a mother, do you sometimes feel like you are a failure? Do you lose your patience and then feel shame for being harsh with your child? Take a deep breath and move forward. Think on ways you can respond to your child without losing your cool. Ask other moms for support and advice that works for them. Then give yourself a break, mothering is hard work! (pgs 177-181)

32. Do you find you are on a never-ending cycle of tasks? When something falls through the cracks do you lose your balance and become overwhelmed with guilt? Make a list of the things that fell through the cracks last month and reassess how you can improve on them in the future. Then, give yourself a break; life always throws a few curveballs. (pgs 182-184)

33. Have you given everything, including extra time at home or away from your family, to a job, only to find that you are simply just another number to them? Have you felt the rejection of being replaced by someone younger or cheaper to hire? Discuss how

it changed your perspective about your work life.
(pgs 185-194)

34. How quick are you to fight back when someone
brings a concern to you? Do you think that you
could have diffused a situation, yet you chose not
to? Have you ever considered simply praying and
letting God defend you? Ponder why you think you
feel the need to take the defensive and how better
you might be able to handle that in the future. (pgs
195-198)

35. Do you have moments or seasons where it
feels like life is squeezing you? Do you let your
circumstances dictate your behavior? Do you turn to
God in the difficult times, or do you try to handle
it all on your own? Take a moment this next week,
every time you feel yourself getting impatient,
angry, or frustrated, and quickly ask God to help
you. Take a few deep breaths, and see if that helps
change the way you react to issues. (pgs 199-205)

36. Do you say things to people and immediately
regret it? Do you have trigger words that when
others say them to you they cause your insecurities
to surface? When is a time recently that either
of those things happened? How did it affect you,
and how do you feel you can improve your life by
working on the way you talk to others and what you
allow in your own life? (pgs 206-209)

37. Have you ever felt like you've lost everything? Did you feel you deserved to lose it all? What good came from that situation? Were you given a second chance at life? Discuss how God can use it for your good and how His second chance can or has restored you. (pgs 210-217)

38. When has a woman purposefully sabotaged you? Why do you think she did that? Have you ever wished for another woman's downfall? Talk about your insecurities and the first memory you have of a female purposefully hurting you. Talk about the first memory you have of a female helping you and how that affected you. (pgs 218-229)

39. Do you have friends that you feel you have to cover up your own problems to keep them around? Do you have friends that lift you when you're low and you can be completely authentic with? Name a recent situation when you felt like you were being fake with a friend. Name another when you were honest, and felt heard and valued. (pgs 230-233)

40. How do you think your friendships make you better? Worse? What type of friend are you to the women in your life? Talk briefly about a few friends that have come and gone. Then about a special friend that has stood the test of time. (pgs 234-238)

41. Have you carried around anxiety due to fear? What is it you are afraid of? List something you

fear, yet know that you can't control, then discuss
how accepting you aren't in control could actually
free you from the worry. (pgs 239-247)

42. Do you fear death? Do you fear your loved ones
dying? Have you faced death and lived through it?
How did it change your feelings about dying? (pgs
248-251)

43. Do you have or do you know someone who has an
addiction? How does that affect your relationships?
(pgs 252-266)

44. Do you let your problems define you, or you
define how you will use your problems? Do you
ask for help or offer help to others because of it?
Discuss. (pgs 267-269)

45. Ever had a miracle happen in your life or the life
of a loved one? Had people deny it or gloss over it
like it wasn't a miracle at all? How did that make
you or your loved one feel? (pgs 270-277)

46. Do you believe tragedies happen to everyone?
Have you faced a tragedy of your own? Did you
call out to God for help? Talk about one of your
tragedies and how it changed your life. (pgs
278-292)

47. Looking back over your life, can you pinpoint something that seemed like a misfortune, but actually turned out to be a blessing? Something negative that God used for your best? Reflect on how God has directed your steps. (pgs 293-298)

48. Do you often feel you have roadblocks, or joy-stoppers, in your life? How do you get through them? Do you believe joy is more a gift or a battle? Think on ways you can help promote joy in your own life, and in the lives around you. (pgs 299-303)

49. When you look back over your life, are you ever amazed at all you've been through? Do you wonder how you made it? Do you feel God equipped you with qualities to pull through? Write yourself a compliment on how you made it to where you are today. If you are still going through something right now, write down a compliment to your future self on how proud you are of you ... for making it through. (pgs 304-314)

50. Looking back at your worst moments, do you feel like you would have willingly gone through what you did, if God had asked you to? Do you believe that God brings good out of all situations to those that love Him? What is your testimony? (pgs 315-319)

51. Have you felt like you were climbing an insurmountable uphill battle alone? Do you often

times feel like you are jumping off a plane not knowing who packed your parachute? Think on ways you can give up more control of your fears and anxiety about the future to God. (pgs 320-328)

52. Are you worried when things change? Is it hard for you to let go of what once was and move forward? Try focusing on the control you do have over your life, and not what is outside of your control. (pgs 329-338)

53. Do you find yourself posting on social media for validation? Do your thoughts wander to things that self-gratify, instead of edify? Keep in mind, what you focus on, you act on. Try to focus on positive substance in life like eternal things, people, and relationships. (pgs 339-343)

God can send wonderful women into your life to lift you up and support you through your battles. It's not trendy to give everything to God. For that matter it's not trendy to love God, so it grows more and more difficult to follow Him, unless you've already felt the mighty power of Him in your life. If you haven't already, search Him out today. He can give you a peace that surpasses all understanding and fear.